T0110069

国家汉办/孔子学院总部
Hanban/Confucius Institute Headquarters

Laozi

Collection of Critical Biographies of Chinese Thinkers

(Concise Edition, Chinese-English)

Editors-in-chief: Zhou Xian, Cheng Aimin

Author: Gao Huaping
Translator: Wang Rongpei, Cao Ying, Wang Shanjiang
Expert: Jin Jing

Nanjing University Press

《中国思想家评传》简明读本 - 中英文版 -

主 编 周 宪 程爱民

老 子

著 者／高华平 Gao Huaping
译 者／汪榕培 Wang Rongpei
　　　曹 盈 Cao Ying
　　　王善江 Wang Shanjiang
审 读／金 晶 Jin Jing

南京大学出版社

Editor: Li Haixia
Cover designed by Zhao Qin

First published 2010
by Nanjing University Press
No. 22, Hankou Road, Nanjing City, 210093
www.NjupCo.com

©2010 Nanjing University Press

Chinese Library Cataloguing in Publication Data
The CIP data for this title is on file with the Chinese Library.

ISBN10: 7-305-06607-8(pbk)
ISBN13: 978-7-305-06607-8(pbk)

Books available in the collection

Confucius
《孔子》
978-7-305-06611-5

Laozi
《老子》
978-7-305-06607-8

Emperor Qin Shihuang
《秦始皇》
978-7-305-06608-5

Li Bai
《李白》
978-7-305-06609-2

Cao Xueqin
《曹雪芹》
978-7-305-06610-8

Du Fu
《杜甫》
978-7-305-06826-3

Zhuangzi
《庄子》
978-7-305-07177-5

Sima Qian
《司马迁》
978-7-305-07294-9

Mencius
《孟子》
978-7-305-07583-4

Mozi
《墨子》
978-7-305-07970-2

总序

General Preface

China is one of the cradles of world civilization, enjoying over five thousand years of history. It has produced many outstanding figures in the history of ancient thought, and left a rich philosophical heritage for both the Chinese people and the entire humanity. The fruit of these thinkers was to establish unique schools that over the long course of history have been continuously interpreted and developed. Today much of these thoughts are as relevant as ever and of extreme vitality for both China and the rest of the world. For instance, the ideal of "humaneness" and the concept of "harmony" taught by Confucius, the founder of Confucianism, have been venerated without ceasing by contemporary China as well as other Asian nations.

Ancient Chinese dynasties came and went, with each new dynasty producing its own scintillating system of thought. These rare and beautiful flowers of philosophy are grounded in the hundred schools vying for attention in pre-Qin times and the broad yet deep classical scholarship of Han and Tang times and in the simple yet profound occult learning of the Wei and Jin dynasties together with the entirely rational learning of Song and Ming Neo-Confucianism. The fertile soil of religious belief was Buddhism's escape from the emptiness of the sensual world and Daoism's spiritual cultivation in the search for identification with the immortals. The founders of these systems of thought included teachers, scholars, poets, politicians, scientists and monks—they made great contributions to such disparate cultural fields in ancient China as philosophy, politics, military science, economics, law, handicrafts, science and technology, literature, art, and religion. The ancient Chinese venerated them for their wisdom and for following moral paths, and called them sages, worthies, saints, wise men, and great masters, etc. Their words and writings, and sometimes their life experiences, constitute the rich matter of ancient Chinese thought distilled by later generations. The accomplishments of Chinese thought are rich and varied, and permeate such spiritual traditions as the harmony between humans and nature, the unification of thought and action, and the need for calmness during vigorous action, synthesizing the old and innovating something new.

Nanjing University Press has persisted over the last twenty years in publishing the 200-book series, *Collection of Critical Biographies of Chinese Thinkers*, under the general editorship of Professor Kuang Yaming, late honorary president of Nanjing University. This collection is the largest-scale project of research on Chinese thinking and culture undertaken since the beginning of the twentieth century. It selected more than 270 outstanding figures from Chinese history, composed their biographies and criticized their

中国是世界文明的发源地之一，有五千多年的文明史。在中国古代思想史上，涌现出了许许多多杰出的思想家，为中华民族乃至整个人类留下了丰富的思想遗产。这些思想成果独树一帜，在漫长的历史中又不断地被阐释、被发展，很多思想对于今天的中国乃至世界而言，仍然历久弥新，极具生命力。比如，儒家学派创始人孔子"仁"的理念、"和"的思想，不仅在当代中国，在其他亚洲国家也一直备受推崇。

古代中国朝代更迭，每一个朝代都有灿烂夺目的思想文化。百家争鸣的先秦诸子、博大宏深的汉唐经学、简易幽远的魏晋玄学、尽心知性的宋明理学是思想学术的奇葩；佛教的色空禅悦、道教的神仙修养是宗教信仰的沃土；其他如经世济民的政治、经济理想，巧夺天工的科技、工艺之道，风雅传神、丹青不老的文学艺术……都蕴涵着丰富的思想。这些思想的创造者中有教师、学者、诗人、政治家、科学家、僧人……他们在中国古代的哲学、政治、军事、经济、法律、工艺、科技、文学、艺术、宗教等各个文明领域内贡献巨大。古代中国人尊敬那些充满智慧、追求道德的人，称呼他们为圣人、贤人、哲人、智者、大师等，他们的言论、著作或被后人总结出来的经验构成了中国古代思想的重要内容，在丰富多彩中贯穿着天人合一、知行合一、刚健中和等精神传统，表现出综合创新的特色。

南京大学出版社坚持20余年，出版了由南京大学已故名誉校长匡亚明教授主编的《中国思想家评传丛书》，这套丛书共200部，是中国20世纪以来最为宏大的中国传统思想文化研究工程，选出了中国历史上270余位杰出人物，为他们写传记，

intellectual accomplishments; all in all, it is a rigorous and refined academic work. On this foundation, we introduce this series of concise readers, which provides much material in a simple format. It includes the cream of the crop of great figures relatively familiar to foreign readers. We have done our best to use plain but vivid language to narrate their human stories of interest; this will convey the wisdom of their thought and display the cultural magnificence of the Chinese people. In the course of spiritually communing with these representative thinkers from ancient China, readers will certainly be able to apprehend the undying essence of thoughts of the Chinese people.

Finally, we are deeply grateful for the support from Hanban/Confucius Institute Headquarters, and the experts from home and abroad for their joint efforts in writing and translating this series.

Editors
November, 2009

评论他们的思想成就，是严肃精深的学术著作。在此基础上推出的这套简明读本，则厚积薄发，精选出国外读者相对较为熟悉的伟大人物，力求用简洁生动的语言，通过讲述有趣的人物故事，传达他们的思想智慧，展示中华民族绚烂多姿的文化。读者在和这些中国古代有代表性的思想家的心灵对话中，一定能领略中华民族思想文化生生不息的精髓。

最后，我们衷心感谢国家汉办/孔子学院总部对本项目提供了巨大的支持，感谢所有参与此套丛书撰写和翻译工作的中外专家学者为此套丛书所做的辛勤而卓有成效的工作。

编者

2009年11月

目录
Contents

一 老子其人与《老子》其书

Chapter I   Getting to Know Laozi and *Laozi*

Do you know which two books have been translated most frequently and spread most widely among all the cultural classics in the world today? They are *The Bible* in the West and *Laozi* in China.

Do you want to know the time-honored and profound traditional Chinese thought and culture? If you want to get the profundity of them, you have to know two cultural celebrities in Chinese history. The two celebrities are Confucius in Confucianism and Laozi in Taoism. Confucius, founder of Confucianism, mainly taught human relations and norms of etiquette, which were concerned with educating people on how to be aggressive and how to serve their sovereigns and fathers so that they could have socially acceptable careers. Laozi, founder of Taoism, taught how people should retreat in order to advance, how they should be humble and how they should overcome the hard with the soft so that they could preserve their body and cultivate their nature: "Do nothing and everything will be done."

Like Confucius, Laozi also has an extremely important position and influence in the traditional Chinese thought and culture, but quite different from Confucius' life stories, his is full of mysteries. At the beginning of last century, there emerged in the Chinese academic world the so-called "the Skeptical School of Early Chinese History" and "the Skeptical Thought of Early Chinese History," which were quite dubious about the ancient Chinese history. Many historical figures, events, literature and classics, including Laozi and *Laozi*, were boldly questioned. Some said that Laozi and *Laozi* were born later than Confucius and Mozi, probably in the middle and late Warring States Period (475~221 B.C.) or even in the reign of Emperor Wen (179~158 B.C.) of the Western Han Dynasty; while others denied that there was such a person as Laozi.

Of course, according to most scholars, it is certain that Laozi with his *Laozi* was born in the late Spring and Autumn Period (771~474 B.C.). In the first general history in the form of a series of biographies in China, the *Records of the Grand Historian*, written by Sima Qian, a famous historian in the Western Han Dynasty, there is "The Biography of Laozi and Han Feizi" to record the life of Laozi despite its shortness of only more than 200 characters.

"The Biography of Laozi and Han Feizi" in the *Records of the Grand*

在当今世界浩如烟海的古代文化典籍中，有两本书被翻译的次数最多流传最为广泛：一本是西方的《圣经》，另一本就是中国的《老子》。

如果你想了解历史悠久、博大精深的中国传统思想和文化，有两个中国历史文化名人你必须认识。这两个人，一个是儒家的孔子，另一个则是道家的老子。孔子是儒家学派的创始人，主张仁和礼，教人积极入世，上进有为，事君事父，做一番改造社会的事业；而老子，则是道家（教）的祖宗，他主张自然无为，治国要无为而治，为人要谦卑居下，以柔克刚，以便全身养性，做到"无为而无不为"。

在中国传统的思想文化中，老子虽然和孔子一样，具有极其重要的地位和影响，但史书上关于他的生平事迹记载得极其简单，他的著作中也无一言半语讲到自己的活动，因而人们对他所知甚少。20世纪初期，中国的学术界出现了对中国上古历史广泛质疑的"疑古思潮"，产生了一个"疑古学派"。他们对许多上古历史人物、历史事件以及文献典籍，提出了大胆的怀疑，其中包括老子其人和《老子》其书。他们之中有人认为老子其人和《老子》其书出现比较晚，应该在孔子和墨子之后，可能产生于战国（公元前475~前221年）中后期，或者在西汉的文帝（公元前179~前158年在位）时代；甚至有人否认有老子这个人的存在。

然而，大多数学者的研究是可信的，即老子其人和《老子》这部书出现于中国的春秋（公元前771~前474年）末期。特别是中国西汉时期著名的史学家司马迁著的《史记》中，有一篇《老子韩非列传》，其中就有一部分是关于老子的传记，尽管它的篇幅很短，只有二三百字。

这篇传记明确地告诉人们，老子是中国春秋时期楚国的苦

Historian records that Laozi was a native of Qurenli of Lixiang Town in Ku County in the state of Chu (Ku County was a dependency of the state of Chen in the Spring and Autumn Period. In 478 B.C., the state of Chen was conquered by the state of Chu and Ku County, located in the east of the Luyi County in Henan Province today, thus became the dependency of Chu). Styled Dan, Laozi's family name was Li and his given name was Er. He was the head of the imperial library (historiographer) in the Zhou Dynasty.

Confucius once consulted Laozi. He went to Zhou and consulted Laozi about the rites, and Laozi said, "As for the rites of the Western Zhou you mentioned, the bodies and bones of the people practicing the rites have dissipated, only their words continue to exist. Besides, a gentleman will carry out his ideas when he has the opportunity and will walk like swaying fleabane in the wind when he does not. I've heard that a good merchant hides his best merchandise, and a virtuous gentleman appears slow-witted. Get rid of your overbearing airs and excessive desires as well as your posturing attitude and greed, as they will do you no good. That's all I can tell you."

Confucius returned and said to his disciples, "As for birds, I know that they are able to fly; as for fish, I know they are able to swim; as for beasts, I know they are able to run. But the running beasts can be captured with nets, the swimming fish can be angled with fishing lines, and the flying birds can be caught with arrows. As for dragons, I have no idea how they ascend to heaven by wind and clouds. Today I met Laozi, who's probably a dragon!"

Laozi pursued Tao and virtue, and his aim was to be a hermit rather than gain fame. Laozi was the head of the imperial library of the Zhou Dynasty for a long time. After the death of King Jing of Zhou in 516 B.C., an internal war for the crown broke out between his two sons, Prince Meng and Prince Chao. In the end, Prince Chao was defeated and fled to the state of Chu with the collection of the classics of the Zhou Dynasty. Seeing that Zhou had declined and that the classics had been taken away by Prince Chao, Laozi resigned and left. It is said that when Laozi arrived at the Pass of Zhou, Yin Xi (also called Guan Yin), the official in charge of the Pass, stopped him and said, "Since you are going to live in seclusion, please write your thoughts into a book for me." Laozi had no choice but to write two masterpieces, explaining Tao and virtue in more than 5 000 Chinese characters. Then he left, and nobody knew his whereabouts afterwards.

县厉乡曲仁里人（苦县位于今河南省鹿邑县，春秋时代本属陈国，公元前478年楚国灭亡陈国，苦县成为楚国属地）。姓李，名耳，字聃，是周朝守藏室之史（即管理文化典籍和史书的官吏）。

孔子曾到周朝去，向老子请教关于礼的学问。老子对孔子说："你所说的西周的礼，制作礼的人和他的骨头都已经腐朽成灰了，只有他说的话还在。再说君子得到了时机就去实行自己的主张，没有时机就像蓬草那样随风飘行。我听说，精明的商人会把自己的好商品藏起来，德行高超的君子，外表看起来像个傻子。把你身上的骄傲之气与各种欲望都去掉吧，还有那种气色与过高的志向，这些东西对你没有任何好处。我所能告诉你的，只有这些了。"

孔子回去以后，对他的弟子们感慨说："鸟，我知道它能飞；鱼，我知道它能游；兽，我知道它能跑。奔跑的野兽可以用罗网捕捉，游走的鱼儿可以用丝线钓起，飞翔的鸟儿可以用箭射下。至于龙，我就没法知道它了，它可以乘风浮云飞上天去。我现在见到的老子，大概是条龙吧！"

老子这个人研究道德之术，他的目标是做一个隐士，不要名声。老子在周朝当了很长时间的守藏室之史。公元前516年，周朝的景王去世，他的两个儿子（王子猛和王子朝）为争夺王位打起了内战，结果王子朝失败，带着周朝王室所藏的典籍逃到楚国去了。老子看到周朝日渐衰败，便辞官而去。老子走到周朝的边关，守关官吏叫尹喜（也有人说叫关尹）的，把老子拦下，说："先生从此就要隐遁了，你勉力为我写一本书吧！"老子没有办法，只好为他著书，写了上下两篇，讲述道德之意，一共五千多字，这才离关而去，从此不知去向。

《老子》帛书残片

Remains of Silk-book *Laozi*

二 《老子》文本的几种形态

Chapter II   Stories Behind *Laozi*

The current *Laozi*, also called *Tao Te Ching*, is composed of two parts *Book of Tao* and *Book of Te*. *Tao Te Ching* is with more than 5 000 Chinese characters in 81 chapters. Is this book the one that as Sima Qian said in the *Records of the Grand Historians* "with more than 5 000 Chinese characters explaining Tao and virtue"?

It is not that easy at all to give an answer.

The current version of *Laozi* was compiled by Wang Bi, a famous scholar when he annotated *Laozi*. Wang Bi lived in the Wei Dynasty during the Three Kingdoms Period. His *Commentaries on Laozi* exerted so much influence that it was thought to elucidate the profundity of the book *Laozi*. Therefore, *Laozi* consisting of 81 chapters became the prevalent version for the posterity.

However, seen from the available literature, the text of *Laozi* was not like what it is today before Wang Bi edited it. There is, in fact, a complicated process between the creation of *Laozi* by Laozi and the birth of the current *Laozi*.

As there is no physical evidence, we have no idea about how "more than 5 000 Chinese characters explaining Tao and virtue" looks like. However, it is affirmative that the earliest extant text of *Laozi* had less than 5 000 Chinese characters; in addition, its form and content were not completely identical with those of the current *Laozi*.

The earliest extant text of *Laozi* was written on the bamboo slips, which were unearthed in the Chu tombs of Guodian in Jingmen of Hubei Province in 1993.

In 1993 at Guodian in Jingmen of Hubei Province, when the archeological team excavated a Chu tomb of the middle Warring States Period, they found a document inscribed on the bamboo slips of three different lengths of 32.3, 30.6, and 26.5 centimeters. All the contents on the bamboo slips can be seen in the current *Laozi*. Therefore, when collated, the document was titled *Laozi*. This is the earliest well-known text of *Laozi*, which is generally called the Guodian *Laozi* or the Bamboo-slip *Laozi*.

The Bamboo-slip *Laozi* has three distinct features. The first one is, as

现在的通行本《老子》一书，又叫《道德经》，分为《道经》和《德经》上下两篇，八十一章五千余字。这是否即是司马迁《史记》中说的"著书上下篇，言道德之意五千余言"的那本著作呢？

这个问题不容易回答。

现在通行的《老子》一书，是三国曹魏时代著名的研究老子的学者王弼，在给《老子》作注释的时候编定的。因为王弼的《老子注》的影响很大，大家都觉得它很好地阐发了《老子》的精义，所以这个八十一章的《老子》，就成了后世通行的本子。

但从现有的文献来看，在王弼编定的《老子》之前，《老子》的文本并不是现在这个样子的。从老子本人最初写作的《老子》，到现在通行本的《老子》的形成，这中间其实有一个复杂的过程。

老子当初写成的"道德之意五千言"是怎样的，因为没有实物为证，我们已无法知道。我们今天所能见到的最早的《老子》文本，既没有五千言，它的形式和内容也与通行本不尽相同，这一点是可以肯定的。

今天我们能见到的最早的《老子》文本，是1993年在湖北荆门郭店楚墓出土的、写在竹简上的《老子》文本。

1993年，考古工作者在湖北荆门郭店发掘了一座战国中期的楚墓，墓中有一篇文献，分别抄写在32.3厘米、30.6厘米、26.5厘米三种不同长度的竹简上。简文的内容都见于通行本的《老子》，所以整理者在整理这篇竹简文献时，就将它题名为《老子》。这也就有了世人所知的最早《老子》文本的实物，一般称为郭店《老子》或楚简《老子》。

楚简《老子》具有三个形式上的特点：一是上面所说的，

mentioned above, that it was written on 71 bamboo slips of different lengths in three bundles. Accordingly, the three bundles were referred to as *Laozi* A, *Laozi* B and *Laozi* C respectively. The second feature is that there were only 2 046 Chinese characters on all the bamboo slips, approximately two-fifths of those of the current *Laozi*. The last is that the Bamboo-slip *Laozi* did not have chapter divisions as the current *Laozi* did, nor was it like the Silk-book *Laozi* that was unearthed in a tomb of the early Western Han Dynasty in Changsha of Hunan Province in 1973. The Silk-book *Laozi* put what was written after Chapter 38 of the current *Laozi* at the beginning, that is, *Book of Te* was in the former part while *Book of Tao* was in the latter. To be specific, *Laozi* A, in accordance with the order of content, was approximately equivalent to 20 chapters of the current *Laozi*. *Laozi* B was equivalent to 8 chapters and *Laozi* C 5 chapters (one of the 5 chapters was just a repetition of that in *Laozi* A).

Then, does the Bamboo-slip *Laozi* represent the original *Laozi*? What is the relationship between it and the current *Laozi*? There is no consensus on the answers to these questions in the academic world at present. One view is that the Bamboo-slip *Laozi* represented the original *Laozi*, for it only had over 2 000 Chinese characters and did not have chapter divisions nor was it divided into two parts (i.e., *Book of Tao* and *Book of Te*). Another view is that the Bamboo-slip *Laozi* was incomplete, because the original *Laozi* had two parts (i.e., *Book of Tao* and *Book of Te*) with more than 5 000 Chinese characters while the former was just selected or extracted from the latter.

The two views, of course, were just guesses, which involved the relationship between the Bamboo-slip *Laozi* and the current *Laozi*. However, they did not explain why the two versions were different in appearance. For example, why was the Bamboo-slip *Laozi* written on three bundles of bamboo slips of different lengths? What did the three different lengths stand for?

In some experts' opinions, bamboo slips of different lengths were supposed to illustrate the structure and quality of the Bamboo-slip *Laozi*, because, according to the writing system of the Qin and Han dynasties, they

它分别抄写在长短不同的三组共71枚竹简上，整理者因此就把它们分别称为《老子》甲组、《老子》乙组和《老子》丙组；二是整个三组《老子》的简文加在一起，才2 046字，约相当于通行本《老子》的五分之二；三是楚简《老子》的内容既没有像通行本《老子》那样分章，也不像1973年在湖南长沙西汉早期墓葬中出土的帛书《老子》那样，把通行本第三十八章以下的内容抄写在全篇的前面，形成了所谓《德经》在前、《道经》在后的情形。具体而言，楚简《老子》甲组内容，按照顺序约相当于通行本共二十章的内容；楚简《老子》乙组内容，按顺序约相当于通行本共八章的内容；楚简《老子》丙组约相当于通行本共五章的内容（而且有一章还与楚简《老子》甲组重复）。

那么，郭店楚简《老子》是否就代表了当时《老子》一书的原貌？它与今天通行本《老子》的关系如何呢？对于这些问题，目前学术界还没有一致的看法。一种看法认为，楚简《老子》代表了早期《老子》的原貌，它只有二千余字，不分章，也不分上下篇（即《道经》与《德经》）；另一种看法认为，楚简《老子》不是完整的《老子》一书，《老子》原书有上下篇（即《道经》与《德经》）共五千字，而楚简《老子》只是五千字《老子》的选本或节抄本。

当然，这两种看法都只是一种推测，涉及到了楚简《老子》和通行本《老子》的关系问题，但并没有说明楚简《老子》为什么会和通行本《老子》的面貌不同。如楚简《老子》为什么要抄写在三组长短不同的竹简上？竹简的长短代表了什么意义？

有专家认为，楚简《老子》之所以要分别抄写在三组长短不同的竹简上，应包含有说明楚简《老子》文章的结构和性质的用意。因为根据秦汉的书写制度，竹简的不同长度是具有区

were used to distinguish the content and quality of the writing. As Zheng Xuan said, the Confucian Five Classics—the *Book of Changes,* the *Book of Documents,* the *Book of Poetry,* the *Book of Rites* and the *Spring and Autumn Annals*—were all written on 2.4-foot-long bamboo slips. For the purpose of modesty, the *Book of Filial Piety* was written on 1.2-foot-long bamboo slips while the *Analects* was on even shorter bamboo slips (only 8 inches) because it was just a record of words and deeds of Confucius and his disciples. When Zhu Xi of the Song Dynasty compiled *Variorum Edition of the Four Books,* he extracted the *Great Learning* from the *Book of Rites* and made a commentary, which was referred to as the *Interpretation of the Great Learning.* In it, Zhu Xi divided the *Great Learning* into two parts. One part, called "Classic," was Confucius' words recorded by Zeng Shen, one of Confucius' disciples. The other part was called "Commentaries," which was Zeng Shen's explanation recorded by his disciple. We give our thanks to Zhu Xi, otherwise, how could we know there are "Classic and Commentaries," two different qualities in such a short article as the *Great Learning*?

The Bamboo-slip *Laozi* was written on three bundles of bamboo slips of different lengths—*Laozi* A, B and C respectively. Likewise, this surely means that the authors and qualities of the Chinese characters on the slips were not the same. The bamboo slips of *Laozi* A were the longest, and the articles should belong to "Classic," which seemed to be written by Laozi himself. The bamboo slips of *Laozi* B and C were shorter than those of *Laozi* A, and the authors should be Laozi's disciples or their pupils. At least, it can be explained in this way according to the shape and structure of the Bamboo-slip *Laozi.* In terms of the statements, conjunctions were used before maxims in each paragraph of *Laozi* B and C. These conjunctions included "*gu,*" "*guyue,*" "*shiwei*" and "*shiyi,*" denoting causality. It seems as if this intentionally showed the relationship between the paragraph and the maxim— explaining and being explained. *Laozi* B and C explained the structure and quality of "Classic" and "Commentaries."

Later than the Bamboo-slip *Laozi* was *Laozi* once quoted by *Zhuangzi* and *Han Feizi.*

There are many records about Laozi in *Zhuangzi,* which can be mainly seen in chapters such as "The Normal Course for Rulers and Kings," "Knowledge Rambling in the North," "The Full Understanding of Life," "Heaven and Earth," "Letting Be and Exercising Forbearance," "Kings Who Have Wished to Resign the Throne," "Cutting Open Satchels," "Metaphorical Language," "Geng-Sang Chu" and "The World." Some of these chapters use

别书写内容和性质的意义的。如郑玄说，儒家的《易》、《书》、《诗》、《礼》、《春秋》"五经"就都抄写在二尺四寸长的竹简上；《孝经》为了表示谦虚，就写在一尺二寸的竹简上，《论语》只是孔子和他的弟子的言行录，书写的竹简就更短些，只有八寸长。宋代的朱熹在编撰《四书章句集注》时，曾将《礼记》中的《大学》一篇抽出来作注，叫《大学章句》。朱熹在《大学章句》中明确地把《大学》一篇分为两个部分，一部分出自孔子之口，而为孔子的弟子曾参所记述——这部分朱熹称为"经"；另一部分则是曾参的解说，而由曾参的弟子所记录——这一部分叫作"传"。幸亏朱熹告诉我们，不然的话，我们怎么会知道在一篇短短的《大学》里面，还有"经"和"传"两种性质的不同呢？

同样的道理，楚简《老子》分别书写在甲、乙、丙三组长度不一的竹简上，应该意味着这三组文字的性质和著作人是不一样的。甲组竹简最长，文章的性质应该属于"经"，它的著作权似应归于老子本人；乙组和丙组竹简要短于甲组，其著作权则应为老子的弟子或再传弟子。至少从楚简《老子》的形制上看，是可以这么说的。而从语句上看，楚简《老子》乙、丙两组中每段的表达方式，都在格言前用"故"、"故曰"、"是谓"、"是以"等表示因果关系的连词连接，似乎有意在表明与甲组的关系是一种解说与被解说的关系——该篇属于解说"经"的"传"的结构和性质。

在楚简《老子》之后，我们能看到的是曾被《庄子》和《韩非子》两书所引用的《老子》。

在《庄子》一书中，有关老子的记载很多，主要见于《应帝王》、《知北游》、《达生》、《天地》、《在宥》、《让王》、《胠箧》、《寓言》、《庚桑楚》、《天下》等篇。其中有些篇中用"老子曰"、

"Laozi said," "Lao Dan said" or "Hence it is said," which obviously indicates that *Laozi* were quoted.

All these quotations can be found in the current *Laozi*, but not all of them in the Bamboo-slip *Laozi*. For example, "The Normal Course for Rulers and Kings" quotes, "Lao Dan said, ' In the governing of the intelligent kings, their services overspread all under the sky, but they do not seem to consider it as proceeding from themselves; their transforming influence reaches to all things, but the people do not refer it to them with hope,' " which can be seen in Chapter 77 of the current *Laozi*—"He works without claiming credit; he succeeds without dwelling upon it; the sage desires no desire." However, there are no such records in the Bamboo-slip *Laozi*. "Cutting Open Satchels" quotes, "In accordance with this it is said, ' As fish never leaves deep waters, so national strategies should not be revealed.' " The same content can be found in Chapter 36 of the current *Laozi* rather than the Bamboo-slip *Laozi*. "Hence it is said, ' The greatest art is like stupidity' " can be seen in Chapter 45 of the current *Laozi* and *Laozi* C. "He who loves his country as he loves his own self can be entrusted to govern the country; he who surrenders his body in service to his country can be its entrusted governor" can be seen in both Chapter 13 of the current *Laozi* and *Laozi* C. "Knowledge Rambling in the North" quotes, "Hence it is said, ' He who pursues Tao does less day by day. Less and less is done until nothing is done at all; when nothing is done at all, nothing is left undone' " can also be found in Chapter 48 of the current *Laozi* and *Laozi* C. "Hence it is said, 'Once Tao is lost, virtue arises; once virtue is lost, humaneness arises; once humaneness is lost, righteousness arises; once righteousness is lost, propriety arises. Propriety signifies the loss of loyalty and faith; it is the beginning of disorder' " appears in Chapter 38 of the current *Laozi* instead of the Bamboo-slip *Laozi*. Some statements in the current *Laozi* have their counterparts in *Zhuangzi*, but they are not completely identical. However, the Bamboo-slip *Laozi* has no such statements at all.

According to these materials, the version of *Laozi* available to Zhuangzi is supposed to be a text with more content than the Bamboo-slip *Laozi* and it is closer to the current *Laozi*.

Slightly later than *Zhuangzi*, Han Feizi, a legalist of the Warring States Period, compiled *Han Feizi*, two chapters of which were entitled "Explaining Laozi" ("Jie Lao") and "Illustrating Laozi" ("Yu Lao"). "Explaining Laozi" ("Jie Lao") explained the meaning of *Laozi* and this was regarded as the beginning of the specific commentary to *Laozi* in the history of Chinese philosophy. "Illustrating Laozi" ("Yu Lao") developed the philosophical

"老聃曰"或"故曰"等，标明是引用了《老子》的话。

《庄子》中所引用的《老子》之言，在通行本《老子》中都可找到，但在楚简《老子》中则有的有，有的没有。如《应帝王》引"老聃曰：明王之治，功盖天下而似不自己，化贷万物而民弗恃"见于通行本第七十七章，作："圣人为而不恃，功成而不处，以其不欲见贤。"但楚简《老子》中却没有类似的话。《胠箧》引"故曰：鱼不可脱于渊，国之利器不可以示人。"同样的内容见于通行本《老子》第三十六章，但楚简《老子》却没有。"故曰：大巧若拙"见于通行本《老子》第四十五章，楚简《老子》乙组也有。"故贵以身为天下，则可以托于天下，爱以身为天下，则可以寄天天下"见于通行本第十三章，又见于楚简《老子》乙组。《知北游》引"故曰：为道者日损，损之又损之，以至于无为，无为而无不为也"见于通行本《老子》第四十八章，又见于楚简《老子》乙组。"故曰：失道而后德，失德而后仁，失仁而后义，失义而后礼。礼者，道之华，而乱之首也"见于通行本第三十八章，而楚简《老子》却没有。还有些通行本《老子》中的句子，《庄子》中也有相似的内容，但二者并不完全相同，而楚简《老子》中也没有。

根据这些材料来看，庄子所见到的《老子》，应该是一种比楚简《老子》内容要多、也更接近于通行本《老子》的文本。

稍晚于《庄子》，战国法家著作《韩非子》中有两篇专门解说《老子》的文章，一篇叫《解老》，另一篇叫《喻老》。《解老》就是解释《老子》的意思，这是中国哲学史上专门解释《老子》的开始。《喻老》就是用历史故事和民间传说阐发

thought of *Laozi* by using historical stories and folklore.

Eleven chapters of *Laozi* quoted in "Explaining Laozi" in *Han Feizi* can be found in the current *Laozi* while twelve chapters in "Illustrating Laozi." Both "Explaining Laozi" and "Illustrating Laozi" only interpreted the extracted sentences. Therefore, it is quite hard to probe into the original text of *Laozi* seen by Han Feizi according to these two articles. However, through the comparison among *Laozi* quoted in the two articles, the Bamboo-slip *Laozi* and the current *Laozi*, *Laozi* available to Han Feizi has some remarkable characteristics.

In the first place, unlike the current *Laozi*, *Laozi* of the time did not have chapter divisions, nor was it sequenced because *Laozi* quoted in "Explaining Laozi" and "Illustrating Laozi" did not cite the current *Laozi* in accordance with its chapter divisions. Though some quotations were comparatively complete, they were not entirely quoted according to the sentence order of the current *Laozi*. This shows that *Laozi* used by Han Feizi was supposed to be a text that did not have chapter divisions yet. In addition, the sentence order of each paragraph was not completely identical with that of the current *Laozi*.

In the second place, of the quotations in "Explaining Laozi" and "Illustrating Laozi," only four chapters of the current *Laozi* can be found in *Laozi* A, three in *Laozi* B and one in *Laozi* C. Also, the sentence order of the quotations was different from that of the Bamboo-slip *Laozi*. This shows that the text of *Laozi* available to Han Feizi should be longer than the Bamboo-slip *Laozi* and the sentence order of them was also different.

There are four kinds of texts of *Laozi* in the Han Dynasty recorded in "Treatise on Literature" of the *Book of Han*, written by Ban Gu, a historian. They are "*Lin's Classic and Commentaries of Laozi*" (in 4 parts), "*Fu's Classic and Commentaries of Laozi*" (in 37 parts), "*Xu's Classic and Commentaries of Laozi*" (in 6 parts) and Liu Xiang's "*Commentaries on Laozi*" (in 4 parts). "Commentaries" in the above books means explanation. However, it cannot be proved or discussed here, for all the books were already lost. The title of Liu Xiang's *Commentaries on Laozi* did not cover the "Classic" text of *Laozi*. So,

《老子》的哲学思想。

在《韩非子》的《解老》篇里，所引用的《老子》，涉及到通行本的有十一章；《喻老》篇所引用的《老子》的内容，涉及通行本《老子》的有十二章。《解老》和《喻老》采用的都是一种摘句式的解释方式，因此，很难根据这两篇来探讨韩非所见《老子》的原貌。但由这两篇引用的《老子》，与楚简《老子》以及通行本《老子》比较来看，韩非写作《解老》、《喻老》时所见的《老子》，有一些不同于通行本《老子》和楚简《老子》的显著特点。

首先，当时的《老子》没有像通行本那样分章和排序，因为《解老》、《喻老》中所引的《老子》，并没有按通行的章次引用《老子》；即使那些较完整地引用了通行本《老子》某章的地方，也没有完全按通行本的语句顺序引用《老子》。这说明韩非所采用的《老子》文本，应该是一个还没有分章，并且各段落的语句的顺序也与通行本不尽相同的本子。

其次，《解老》和《喻老》中引用的《老子》，只有通行本中的三章的内容见于楚简《老子》甲组，有四章的内容见于楚简《老子》乙组，另有一章见于楚简《老子》丙组。而两篇所引《老子》的文句次序，也与楚简《老子》不同。这说明，韩非所见到的《老子》文本，应该比楚简《老子》篇幅要大，顺序也不相同。

汉代的《老子》文本，历史学家班固的《汉书·艺文志》中记载了四种，它们分别是"《老子邻氏经传》四篇"、"《老子傅氏经说》三十七篇"、"《老子徐氏经说》六篇"、"刘向《说老子》四篇"。以上几种书中的"说"，同"传"一样，都是解说的意思。只是它们都已经亡佚，无法据实加以讨论了。推测起来，刘向《说老子》四篇，题目上不包括《老子》"经"文，

the quotations in it were presumably supposed to be similar to those in "Explaining Laozi" and "Illustrating Laozi" and they were the extracted sentences. The titles of the other three books contained not only "Classic" but also "Commentaries." It is self-evident that the "Classic" text and the "Commentaries" were combined. There is just no way to know whether the combination was like "Classic" and "Commentaries" in the *Great Learning*, which put the entire "Classic" text of *Laozi* before the "Commentaries," or like "Explaining Laozi" and "Illustrating Laozi," which divided the "Classic" text into one, two or several sentences before the explanation.

The most featured and well-preserved are two texts of *Laozi* of the Han Dynasty, which were not recorded by "Treatise on Literature" of the *Book of Han*. One is the Silk-book *Laozi* (identified simply as Transcript "A" and Transcript "B"), unearthed in an ancient tomb of the Western Han Dynasty at Mawangdui in Changsha of Hunan Province in 1973. The other one is Heshanggong's *Commentaries on Laozi*.

In the winter of 1973, two transcripts of *Laozi* were unearthed in Mawangdui No. 3 tomb in Changsha of Hunan Province. One of them was referred to as Transcript "A" written in seal characters. The other one was called Transcript "B" written in Li scripts. Transcript "A" did not avoid the name taboo of Emperor Liu Bang of the Han Dynasty, which shows that it was copied before Liu Bang established his empire. Transcript "B" avoided the name taboo of Liu Bang rather than that of Liu Heng, Emperor Wen, which shows that it was copied after Liu Bang proclaimed himself emperor and before Liu Heng succeeded to the throne. Both Transcript "A" and Transcript "B" were produced at the beginning of the Western Han Dynasty.

Transcript "A" distinguishes from Transcript "B" in some aspects, such as the sentence structure, functional words, ancient and modern Chinese characters and phonetic loan characters throughout the "Classic" text. Compared with the Bamboo-slip *Laozi* and the current *Laozi*, the silk transcripts have some remarkable characteristics.

For one thing, the Silk-book *Laozi* corresponded with the current *Laozi* in Chinese characters and length. In contrast with *Laozi* quoted by *Zhuangzi* and *Han Feizi*, Chinese characters were largely increased in the Silk-book *Laozi*, which shows that the text of *Laozi* took shape at that time. Therefore, chances are that the texts of *Laozi* of later ages only made some changes on individual Chinese characters rather than whole paragraphs or sentences.

其中引用《老子》，应该同韩非的《解老》和《喻老》相近，属于摘句式的。"《老子邻氏经传》四篇"、"《老子傅氏经说》三十七篇"、"《老子徐氏经说》六篇"，题目上就既有"经"，也有"传"（或"说"）。可见，这几种书中是"经"文和"传"（或"说"）文结合在一起的。只是不知道这种结合，是否如《大学》中的"经"和"传"那样，先把《老子》"经"文全部列出，"经"文后面全部都是"传"文；还是如《解老》和《喻老》那样，把《老子》"经"文分成几句或一两句，分别加以解说。

汉代的《老子》文本，最有特色而且较完整地保存下来的，是《汉书·艺文志》并没有著录的两种本子。一种是1973年在湖南长沙马王堆西汉古墓中出土的帛书《老子》甲、乙本，另一种就是西汉时的河上公注本《老子》。

1973年冬天，在湖南长沙马王堆三号汉墓出土了两种《老子》抄本。其中一种用篆书抄写，称为甲本；另一种用隶书抄写，称为乙本。甲本不避汉代皇帝刘邦的名讳，说明它抄写在刘邦正式称帝建国之前；乙本避刘邦的名讳，但不避汉文帝刘恒的名讳，说明它写定在刘邦称帝之后，刘恒继位之前，都属于西汉初年的作品。

帛书《老子》甲、乙本在经文句型、虚词以及所用古今字和假借字等方面均有差别。而它们与楚简《老子》及通行本《老子》相比，也有一些明显的特点。

第一，帛书《老子》文本，已有通行本《老子》的字数与篇幅，这与楚简本以及《庄子》、《韩非子》所引用的《老子》相比，字数已经有了很大的增加。这说明当时的《老子》文本已经基本定型，后世的《老子》文本只可能有个别文字的变动，而不是整段甚至整句的增减。

For another thing, unlike the current *Laozi*, the Silk-book *Laozi* did not have chapter divisions. Instead, it divided the text into two parts, with *Book of Te* in the former part and *Book of Tao* in the latter. This was a further development for the texts of *Laozi* of the pre-Qin period, among which the text of the Bamboo-slip *Laozi* was a representative. It is shown that along with the constant enrichment and improvement of the contents of the texts of *Laozi*, the preliminary arrangements and adjustments of the structure of them have been made.

Another text of the Han Dynasty, which played a key role in the development of the texts of *Laozi*, is Heshanggong's *Commentaries on Laozi*.

"The Bibliography of Chronicles" of the *Book of Sui Dynasty* records that Heshanggong lived in the time of Emperor Wen (179~156 B.C.) of the Western Han Dynasty and annotated *Laozi*. Heshanggong's *Commentaries on Laozi* we mentioned above is just the text of *Laozi* preserved in Heshanggong's *Commentaries on Laozi*.

Commentaries on *Laozi* were also made in the Western Han Dynasty prior to Heshanggong. For example, there is Yan Zun's *Laozi Annotations*, whose original text was unfortunately lost. It is hard to identify its original appearance, even though there were some extracted materials from other books. However, Heshanggong's *Commentaries on Laozi* was completely preserved, which is of help to our comprehension of its characteristics.

There are two most obvious features in Heshanggong's *Commentaries on Laozi*.

In the first place, Heshanggong's *Commentaries on Laozi* divided *Laozi* into 81 chapters for the first time. Part one, comprising chapter 1~37, was known as *Book of Tao* while chapter 38~81 made up *Book of Te*. Also, each chapter was given a subtitle (at least it can be seen from the Song Dynasty block-printed edition). For example, the first chapter was titled "Embodying the Tao," the second "The Nourishment of the Person," the third "Keeping the People at Rest," the fourth "The Fountainless," ... the eightieth "Standing Alone" and the eighty-first "The Manifestation of Simplicity." This chapter division became the standard for all the texts of *Laozi* of later ages. Though the subtitles have not been adopted by the current *Laozi*, it, undoubtedly, largely contributes to readers' understanding of the gist of each chapter of *Laozi*.

第二，帛书《老子》没有如通行本《老子》那样的分章，而只是将全篇分为《道经》和《德经》两部分，《德经》居前而《道经》居后。这是对以楚简《老子》为代表的先秦《老子》文本的进一步发展。它说明随着《老子》文本内容的不断丰富和完善，人们已对《老子》文本的结构做出了初步的安排与调整。

汉代另一个在《老子》文本发展过程中具有重要地位的本子，是河上公注本《老子》。

河上公这个人，《隋书·经籍志》说他是汉文帝（公元前179~前156年在位）时代的人，曾给《老子》作注。我们所说的河上公注本《老子》，就是指保存在河上公《老子注》中的《老子》文本。

在河上公之前，西汉也有人给《老子》作过注解，比如说有严遵的《老子注》。可惜，原书已经散佚，根据后人从别的书中摘录来的材料，已很难看出它的原貌。但河上公的《老子注》完整地保存下来了，有利于我们来认识它的特点。

河上公注本《老子》有两个特点最为明显。

首先，河上公注《老子》文本，第一次把整篇《老子》划分为八十一章，其中第一章至第三十七章为《道经》；第三十八章到第八十一章为《德经》。而且，河上公注《老子》文本还给从第一章到第八十一章的每一章加上了标题（至少现在可以看到的宋代的刻本是这样的）。如第一章为"体道"，第二章叫"养身"，第三章为"安民"，第四章叫"无源"……第八十章为"独立"，第八十一章叫"显质"。这种分章成为了以后所有《老子》文本的标准样式；而为每章安上标题虽然不为通行本《老子》所吸取，但却无疑十分有利于读者理解《老子》每章的大意。

In the second place, like the Silk-book *Laozi*, Heshanggong's *Commentaries on Laozi* also divided *Laozi* into two parts. However, in contrast with the Silk-book, Heshanggong's *Commentaries on Laozi* began with *Book of Tao*. The current *Laozi* inherited this structural pattern.

By the late Han Dynasty and the Wei and Jin dynasties, a trend of talking about the metaphysics emptily had spread across the width and breadth of the Chinese academic world, which developed into the metaphysical thought (*Xuanxue*). One of the founders of the metaphysics was Wang Bi of the Cao and Wei dynasties, who wrote the *Commentaries on Laozi*, which was established as the current *Laozi*.

Styled Fusi, Wang Bi (226~249 A.D.) was from Shanyang (in the Jinxiang County of Shandong Province today). He was discovered by He Yan (190~249 A.D.), the Minister of the Ministry of Personnel of the time, and they both became representatives of the metaphysics during the Zhengshi Period (239~249 A.D.). Both of them annotated *Laozi*. Thus, ranking equally with the *Book of Changes* and *Zhuangzi*, *Laozi* became one of the three books that metaphysicians must read (the three were referred to as the "Three Metaphysics"). Wang Bi's *Commentaries on Laozi* became the current *Laozi* from then on. As a result, the text of *Laozi* finally took shape. Written in more than 5 000 Chinese characters, the text consists of 81 chapters without subtitles, with *Book of Tao* in the former part and *Book of Te* in the latter.

Each text of *Laozi* is different in the ideological content, but merely the evolution of the external forms and structures has presented many complicated stories.

On the other hand, there are, of course, different texts of *Laozi* in history and people's interpretations of the book are not completely identical. However, when we are talking about *Laozi* today, we can only base our discussions on the more stereotyped text. Because before that there is enough evidence to prove that the original *Laozi* is not like this, only this text of *Laozi* can more comprehensively and fully show Laozi's ideological connotations.

其次，河上公注《老子》文本，不仅如帛书本《老子》那样，把整篇《老子》分为《道经》和《德经》上下两篇，而且还把帛书《老子》的《德经》居前而《道经》居后的结构形式，改成了《道经》在前而《德经》在后的形式。通行本《老子》也继承了这种结构模式。

到汉末和魏晋时期，中国学术界兴起了清谈玄虚的风气，后来发展成为玄学思潮。这种玄学思潮的创立者之一，就是曹魏时期因给《老子》作注而成为通行本《老子》文本的确立者王弼。

王弼（公元226~249年），字辅嗣，山阳人（今属山东金乡）。他被当时任吏部尚书的何晏（公元190~249年）发现，一起成为了曹魏正始年间（公元239~249年）玄学的代表。他们都为《老子》作了注解，使《老子》和《周易》、《庄子》并列，成为玄学家必读的三本书（称为"三玄"）。而王弼注释的《老子》文本，更成为了后世通行的《老子》文本。一个全书由《道经》和《德经》上、下两篇构成，《道经》在前、《德经》在后，共分为无标题的八十一章、五千余字的《老子》文本，最终定型了。

尽管《老子》的每种文本形态都包含着思想内容上的差异，但仅仅是这些外在形式结构的演变，就已经向我们讲述了许许多多曲折的故事。

后来的整理者总会加进去一些并非老子原始思想的资料，每个人对《老子》一书的解读也并不完全相同，但我们今天谈《老子》，仍只能以这个最后趋于定型的《老子》文本作依据。因为在没有确实的证据证明最初的《老子》完全不是这样的情况下，只有现在通行的这个《老子》文本，才能向我们更全面、更充分地展示老子的思想内涵。

老子骑牛图
Picture of Laozi on an Ox

三 老子思想的来源

Chapter Ⅲ   The Source of Laozi's Thought

1. The Outcome of Social Change

Laozi was born in the late Spring and Autumn Period, which marked a transition from the slavery society to the feudalist one in China. This was not only a period of great changes and turmoil in politics and economy, but also a time of "the collapse of propriety and music." Laozi's thought was a product of this era.

The political and social changes in the Spring and Autumn Period in China were attributable primarily to the improvement in productivity, which was mainly reflected by the rapid growth in the agricultural production. The symbol of the agricultural production was the widespread use of iron farming tools and the popularity of the ox plough technology. Books by the pre-Qin scholars record many iron farming tools, such as spade-shaped farming tools in *Guanzi* and iron pots in *Mozi*. "Yongye" of the *Analects* records what Confucius said, "The calf of an ox is red and has good horns." It also records that the given name of his disciple Ran Boniu (ox) was Geng (plough) and Sima Ziniu was also styled Geng (plough). The joint name of ox and plough (niu and geng in Chinese) shows that the ox plough was used widely at the time. Therefore, "Discourses of Jin" of *Guoyu* (*Remarks of Monarchs*) says, "The feudal clans, Fan and Zhongxing of the state of Jin, were not considerate of the populace. They only desired for the political power of the state. Consequently, their descendants were expelled out of Jin and did ploughing in the state of Qi. The noble sacrifices in the temples in the past had to toil in the fields." All these demonstrate the popularity of the ox plough.

The popularity of the iron farming tools and ox plough, in turn, boosted the development of the economy in agricultural production and led to the changes in the economic system and social structure.

A large amount of wasteland was opened up in the Spring and Autumn Period. With the increase of private land, there were more and more land-holding farmers. The vassal states, one after another, changed the form of exploitation—collecting land taxes and levies instead of tribute and taxes. The states of Lu, Chu and Qin conducted similar reforms.

The social and political changes were reflected, on the one hand, in the decentralized national power, and on the other hand, in the constant annexations among the vassal states.

At the beginning of the Western Zhou Dynasty, the Son of Heaven of

（一）社会巨变的产物

老子生活的时代，是中国春秋末期。这是中国社会由奴隶制社会向封建制社会转变的时期，是一个政治、经济大变革大动荡的时期，也是一个"礼崩乐坏"的时期。老子的思想就是这个时代的产物。

春秋时期中国社会政治、经济的变革，首先来自生产力的提高。而当时社会的生产力的提高，又主要表现为农业生产的迅速发展，其标志是铁制农具的广泛使用和牛耕技术的普及。先秦诸子的书中记载了许多的铁制农具，如《管子》中的铁耜、《墨子》中的铁镬等。《论语·雍也》篇中，孔子说："犁牛的儿子长着赤色的毛，整齐的角。"孔子的另一些弟子冉耕字伯牛，司马耕字子牛。将"牛"与"犁"、"牛"与"耕"作人的名与字，说明当时的牛耕的确已经很普遍。所以《国语·晋语（九）》说："晋国当时的卿大夫范氏和中行氏不懂得体恤百姓，想独揽晋国的政权，结果弄得他们的子孙被人赶出了晋国，到齐国做耕田的农夫去了，往日宗庙高贵的祭品（牛），如今去承担田间耕田的辛劳了。"这都说明了牛耕的普遍。

铁制农具的普及和牛耕的推广，带动了农业生产的发展，带动了社会经济制度和社会结构的变化。

由于大量的荒地得到了开垦，私田迅速增多，出现了很多自耕农。各诸侯国也相继改变剥削方式，把收贡赋改成了按田亩数收取租税。如当时的鲁国、楚国、秦国，都曾做过类似的改革。

社会政治方面的变革，一是表现为国家政权的下移，二是表现为诸侯的兼并战争不断。

西周初年的时候，周天子采用"分封制"管理天下。所谓

Zhou administered the nation by the "system of enfeoffment" (to invest somebody with the freehold possession of a piece of land). The so-called "system of enfeoffment" means that the Son of Heaven of Zhou conferred the land and population to his brothers and relatives, who thus became dukes. Then, the dukes conferred their land and population to their brothers and relatives, who thus became feudal clans. Likewise, the clans bestowed their brothers and relatives as vassals.

In the Spring and Autumn Period, the nation was out of the control of the Son of Heaven of Zhou that was reduced to a trifle one, only occupying the capital city—a small territory. In contrast, big vassal states, such as the states of Qi, Jin, Qin, Chu, Wu and Yue gained the dominant position one after another and issued orders to the world. However, the politics and economy inside these vassal states were actually under control of the more powerful feudal clans, such as Bao, Cui, Qing and Chen of the state of Qi, Fan, Zhongxing, Zhi, Xun, Zhao, Wei and Han of the state of Jin. As a consequence, big events happened, such as "The House of Tian Sent a Punitive Expedition against the State of Qi" and "The Houses of Zhao, Wei and Han Carved Up the State of Jin." This situation is precisely recorded in the "The Grand Historian's Preface" of the *Records of the Grand Historian*, "The Spring and Autumn Period witnessed 36 cases of rulers being killed and the destruction of 52 vassal states. There were innumerable cases regarding the dukes in exile, whose thrones could not be maintained."

In this political situation, the overlords who contended for dominance on the political stage always extorted heavy taxes and levies. They were extravagant and dissipated, excessively indulging themselves in lewdness and lived as if in intoxication or dreams. In contrast, the populace either became homeless, wandering from place to place, or rose in revolt and became "bandits" in every corner. In terms of the cultural system, the so-called situation of "the collapse of propriety and music" was thus created.

"The collapse of propriety and music" means that the original cultural rules of propriety and music of the Western Zhou Dynasty did not work and were badly damaged. In the cultural system of the Western Zhou Dynasty, a set of principles of the hierarchical relationship between individuals were established corresponding to the system of enfeoffment in politics. For example, "there should be righteousness between the sovereign and the ministers, affection between the father and the son, attention to separate functions between the husband and the wife, a proper order between the old and the young and fidelity between friends." The "Three Rites" of the

"分封制"，就是周天子把天下的土地和人民分封给自己的子弟和亲戚，这些子弟和亲戚就成为诸侯；诸侯再把自己的封地和人民分给自己的子弟和亲戚，这些子弟和亲戚就成了卿大夫；卿大夫如法炮制，把自己子弟和亲戚分封为家臣。

春秋时期，周天子失去了对天下的控制，仅保存了京城地区的一小块地盘，降为微不足道的小国，而诸侯大国如齐、晋、秦、楚、吴、越则先后称霸，号令天下。而各诸侯国之内那些强劲的卿大夫，例如齐国的鲍氏、崔氏、庆氏、陈氏，晋国的范氏、中行氏、智氏、荀氏、赵氏、魏氏、韩氏等，实际上控制着本国的政治与经济，诸侯父子兄弟相杀争权，卿大夫夺权，最终演成了"田氏代齐"、"三家分晋"等重大事件。司马迁在《史记·太史公自序》中说："在春秋这段历史之中，发生了国君被杀的事件三十六起，被消灭的诸侯国有五十二个，至于诸侯王逃亡在外、王位不保的，就数也数不清了。"

在这种政治局面下，那些霸主们横征暴敛、奢侈腐化、荒淫无度、醉生梦死；而老百姓则或流离失所，或揭竿而起，成为遍地的"盗贼"。而从文化制度方面来说，这就出现了所谓"礼崩乐坏"的局面。

所谓"礼崩乐坏"，是指当时社会中原有的西周的礼乐文化制度遭到了严重的破坏。西周时期，与政治上实行分封制相应，在文化制度方面也建立起一套规范人与人之间等级关系的原则。如"君臣有义，父子有亲，夫妇有别，长幼有序，朋友有信"等等。儒家经典中的"三礼"（指《周礼》、《仪礼》、

Confucianist classics (*Rites of Zhou, Etiquette and Rites* and the *Book of Rites*) collected these types of the institutions handed down from generation to generation. However, by the Spring and Autumn Period, the rules of propriety and music of the Western Zhou Dynasty could not be maintained any longer.

For instance, in 606 B.C., King Zhuang of Chu sent a punitive expedition against the ethnic minority groups in Luhun, but in the end, he deployed his troops in the suburbs of the capital of Zhou, which upset King Ding of Zhou. The king hurriedly sent Wang Sunman to reward King Zhuang. Unexpectedly, King Zhuang asked about the size and weight of the precious tripod of Zhou, which was actually a symbol of the royal power. This showed that King Zhuang had long harbored the thought of "Throne can be taken in turn among us," and looked down upon the so-called "rites of Zhou."

Here is another example. According to the rites of Zhou, the music, *Yong*, would be played only after the Son of Heaven of Zhou offered sacrifices in the ancestral temple. However, Mengsun, Shusun and Jisun, the feudal clans of the state of Lu, also played the music in their homes. Moreover, Jisun even broke the "rites" and had the grand dance accompanied by music (Bayi) in his own yard, which could only be enjoyed by the Son of Heaven of Zhou. The dance was performed by 64 people. This was an astonishing conduct as it was against the rites and over the limit of their rights.

Laozi was a historiographer who showed strong concern for the social reality. The situation is what was described by Laozi, "Tao is absent from the world." In Chapter 75, he said, "The people are starving just because the rulers are guilty of over-taxation and therefore, they are starving." ❶ "The palaces are magnificent, while fields are overgrown with weeds and granaries are empty. Still some people are clad in grand clothes, carry sharp weapons, indulge in grand food, and overflow with excessive wealth. They can properly be called master thieves" (Chapter 53). Laozi revealed the disparity of wealth and pointed out the reason that contributed to the phenomenon that "Man gives to those who have excess."

The unequal distribution of the social and economic wealth inevitably led to the struggles for power, wars for redistribution of the social resources and resistance from the people. The social phenomenon of the time was described

《礼记》三书），就是集中记载他们代代相传的这种典章制度的著作。但是到了春秋时期，西周礼乐制度已经没法维持下去了。

例如，公元前606年，楚庄王讨伐陆浑地方的少数民族，结果跑到了周朝的京郊，陈兵于周朝的京都，弄得周定王十分紧张，忙派王孙满去犒劳楚庄王。而楚庄王竟然问起周王朝宝鼎的大小和轻重来。王室的宝鼎，是王权的象征。楚庄王敢于向周王询问鼎的大小轻重，说明他心里已有"皇帝轮流做"的意思，早已不把所谓"周礼"放在眼里了。

又例如，按照周礼的规定，只有天子在宗庙祭祀完毕才唱《雍》这首乐歌，而鲁国的卿大夫孟孙氏、叔孙氏和季孙氏，在自己家里也唱起了《雍》这首乐歌。并且季孙氏还打破"礼"的规定，把只有天子才能享用的六十四人的乐舞（八佾）搬到家里来了，在自己的庭院里搞起了宏大的表演。这是一种非礼僭越的举动。

老子是一个具有很强烈的现实关怀感的史官，他把这种情形称为"天下无道"。他说："老百姓受饥饿，是因为他们上交的赋税太多了，所以才受饥饿。"❶（第七十五章）"朝廷之上非常污秽，田地一片荒芜，仓库极其空虚，但有权势的人还穿着鲜丽的衣服，佩带宝剑，吃腻了山珍海味，家里的钱财无数，这种行为叫作盗窃和炫耀。"（第五十三章）这是老子对当时贫富悬殊的社会现象进行的揭露，并且深刻地指出了造成这种"损不足以补有余"的社会现象的原因。

诸侯的经济和军事实力强大，必然会导致争权夺利，导致要求重新分配社会资源的战争以及人民的抗争。老子所谓"天

---

❶ 本文以下引《老子》，都只注明章次。

❶ Quotations from *Laozi* later are only documented the chapters.

in "When Tao is absent from the world, it will be filled with chaos and wars, thus colts are bred on the battlefields" (Chapter 46). "Where troop is stationed, thorns and brambles grow. In the sequence of large-scale wars there are sure to be bad years" (Chapter 30). Confronted with such reality, the people were only driven to revolt and became "bandits" who could not be annihilated by rulers. Chapter 74 says, "The people do not fear death; to what purpose is it to (try to) frighten them with death?" All these were actually Laozi's summary of the reality of his time and his reflections on the solution.

Therefore, Laozi was more of a social and historical product of the late Spring and Autumn Period of pain and confusion than a sage and philosopher.

2. The Accumulation of Former Culture

Laozi's thought was not only the product of the social suffering and chaotic reality of the Spring and Autumn Period, but also the outcome of the accumulation of the original ideological culture of the earlier generations.

The thought and wisdom in *Laozi* is very familiar to later generations, such as "advocating the soft and weak," "speaking in modest terms," "giving first what you want to take," "keeping womanly qualities and stressing *yin*" and "enjoying quietness and restraint." However, seen from the source of thought and culture, such wisdoms had been frequently found in the thinking of our nation prior to Laozi.

For example, "The Great Plan" of the *Classic of History* refers to "the soft rule" implied in "being harmonious and soft can ensure success," "correctness and straightforwardness" and "the hard rule" as the "Three Virtues," which are "indispensable to the governing of people." "The Counsels of Gao Yao" of the *Classic of History* also records the version that "being harmonious and soft can ensure success." ❶ This indicates that as early as the Shang Dynasty, people already realized the close relationship between "being soft" and "being harmonious." The approach of "being soft" was a must in securing the

下无道，那么社会就会混乱不堪、战事不断，母马就会在郊外产下马驹"（第四十六章），而"军队驻扎过的地方，就会变成荒野，生长荆棘；发生过一场战争之后，必然会引发饥荒之年"（第三十章）等等，就是老子对这种社会现象的描述。人民在这样的现实面前，只能被迫反抗，揭竿而起，成为统治者杀不胜杀的"强盗"。所谓"老百姓不怕死，为什么还要以处死的方式使他们害怕呢？"（第七十四章）这些，实际都是老子对当时社会现实的概括，以及对这一现实的忧虑。

所以，与其说老子是当时社会的智者与哲人，还不如说他是春秋末期那段痛苦而动乱的社会历史的见证者。他的思想是当时社会巨变的产物。

（二）前代思想文化的积淀

老子思想既是春秋战国之际社会痛苦和混乱现实的产物，同时也是前代原始思想文化积淀的结果。

《老子》一书中的思想智慧有许多为后人所详熟，如崇尚柔弱、谦卑处下、欲取姑与、守雌重阴、好静尚俭等等。但是，如果从思想文化的源头来看，在老子之前，我们民族的思维原本就不乏这样的智慧。

例如，《尚书》的《洪范》篇把"和柔能治"的"柔克"与"正直"、"刚克"一起称为"治民必用"的"三德"；《尚书·皋陶谟》中也有"柔而立"的说法，表示"和柔而能立事"❶。这说明，早在商代，人们就已经认识到"柔"与"和"是密切相关的，要实现人与人之间的和谐，就必须采用柔软的方式，减轻乃至消弥双方的冲突。这种平和柔弱的行

❶《尚书·洪范》孔传，《尚书正义》卷十二。

❶ "The Great Plan," in the *Classical of History*.

harmonious relationship between people so that conflicts could be reduced or even eliminated. This approach contributed not only to one's success but also to the stability and harmony of a nation. Therefore, both *Shuo Yuan* and *Confucius' Sayings Collected for the Family* have a quotation from *Jin Ren Motto*, "A violent person will never die a natural death; an aggressive person will inevitably encounter a strong rival." The first sentence of this motto is also directly quoted from Chapter 42 of *Laozi*. It is shown that Laozi's thinking that people should not try out their new spurs actually inherited the thought of the Shang and Zhou dynasties.

Another example can be found in Chapter 36 of *Laozi*.

> That which is to be reduced must first be expanded; that which is to be weakened must first be strengthened; that which is to be removed must first be accepted; that which is to be taken must first be given. This is called "subtle insight" —the soft and weak overcome the hard and strong.

We have already pointed out the source of Laozi's thought of "advocating the soft and weak," while his opinion "that which is to be taken must first be given" also has its own origin. "Collected Persuasions" of *Han Feizi* records a similar statement in the *Book of Zhou*, which goes like this,

> In order to defeat someone, one should first support it; in order to take something, one should first give it.

As head of the imperial library of the Zhou Dynasty, Laozi was naturally very familiar with the classics of thought and culture of the earlier generations. So, he could easily quote those epigrams. Laozi always made it clear that the epigrams were quoted from ancient books or sayings. Cases in point are "Ancient wisdom declares" in Chapter 41 and "There is a saying among military strategists" in Chapter 69. On the other hand, *Laozi* contains many similar statements, such as "the sage said" and how "the ancient sages who were followers of Tao" behaved. All these statements can actually be regarded as his own reminder that he assimilated and made use of the thought of the forebears.

It can be obviously seen that Laozi assimilated and used the outcome of the ideological culture of earlier generations. In fact, the deeper impact on Laozi's thought was some primitive cultural factors in the early Chinese history and culture, such as "worship of females" and "worship of reproduction."

In the primitive society of the ancient Chinese times, our ancestors had very bad living conditions and low viability. Thus, the reproduction of

为方式，既有利于个人办成事情，也能够把国家治理得安定和谐。所以，《说苑》和《孔子家语》两书中都引述《金人铭》说："强盛横暴的人不得善终，好胜的人一定会遇到强敌。"《老子》一书的第四十二章也直接引用了《金人铭》中的前一句话。这说明，老子强调为人处世不可锋芒太露，实际是对商、周两代思想成果的继承。

又例如，《老子》第三十六章说：

> 将欲歙之，必固张之；将欲弱之，必固强之；将欲去之，必固与之；将欲夺之，必固予之。是谓微明。柔弱胜刚强。

崇尚柔弱的思想根源我们刚才已经指出，而老子的"欲取姑与"的观点，实际是有其本源的。《韩非子》一书的《说林（上）》一篇，就曾记载前代的《周书》中有类似的话：

> 《周书》说："想要打败它，姑且先辅助它，想要夺取它，一定要暂且给予它。"

老子本是周朝的守藏室之史，他对前代的思想文化典籍自然是十分熟悉的，所以他才能对那些思想文化警句随手引来，不露痕迹。老子自己也常常明白地告诉人们，他的著作中引述了古书或古人之言，如《老子》第四十一章中的《建言》有之"，第六十九章的"《用兵》有言"等等。而《老子》一书中的"圣人云"、"古之善为道者"之类的用语也特别多，这些都显示出是老子吸收、利用了前人的思想观念。

当然，以上所说的老子对前代思想文化成果的吸收和利用，都还是比较浅层的，是人们一看便知的。实际上，对老子思想影响更深层的，是中国早期历史文化中的某些原始文化因子，如女性崇拜、生殖崇拜等等。

在中国上古时期的原始社会里，先民的生存条件很差，自

population and the continuation of races became a top priority. Females played a more important role than males in the breeding of children, fruit picking and the feeding of livestock. Naturally, the society of the time was matriarchal, which led to the worship of females. The worship of females created different "Gansheng myths" (women have babies without sex) regarding the ancestral mothers in China. For example, it was said that Fu Xi' mother got pregnant and produced him after stepping into a footprint of Lei Ze—the God of Thunder, that the Yellow Emperor's mother became pregnant with him after witnessing a great flash of lightning, that Jian Di gave birth to Shang Qi after accidentally swallowing a multi-colored swallow's egg, that Jiang Yuan got pregnant and gave birth to Hou Ji after stepping into a footprint of Heaven, and that Nu Wa used yellow clay to create human beings. They were all the outcome of worship of females.

The society in which Laozi lived had long been patriarchal and females' position had already been replaced by males. Despite this, the cultural factors in the worship of females did not vanish; instead, they were accumulated in the deep structure of our national culture and ways of thinking. Some attributes of females' culture can be obviously found in the philosophy of life in Laozi' thinking, such as "advocating the weak and keeping womanly qualities," "stressing *yin* and advocating compassion" and "enjoying quietness and humility."

Laozi said in Chapter 67 that he had three treasures, the first one was compassion, the second was restraint and the third was humility. "Compassion," "restraint" and "humility" actually involved some attributes of females or mothers. "Eight Fallacies" of *Han Feizi* says, "The compassionate mother, in loving her little child, was surpassed by none." The passage said, "The bond of mother and child is love, and the relationship between ruler and minister is expediency." It can be seen that "compassion" is naturally united with "love" and mother's love is the most selfless. Therefore, "compassion" can be regarded as one of the attributes of females' culture. Likewise, "restraint" and "humility" are also related to the nature of females. The reason why Laozi advocated and appreciated these features of females should be related to the cultural tradition of the worship of females hidden in his thinking.

It is also because of this that Laozi gave praise and respect to things with the attributes of femininity or females, such as "water," "void," "quietness"

身的生存能力也很低，因此，人口的繁衍、种族的延续便是当时社会的头等大事。女性在繁育后代、采摘果实、豢养家畜等工作中，发挥着比男性更重要的作用。当时的社会自然地就处于母系社会阶段，由此导致了对女性的崇拜。后世流传的各种女性始祖"感生"的神话，如伏羲氏之母踏雷泽大人之迹感生伏羲，黄帝之母见大电光感生黄帝，简狄吞玄鸟之卵而生（商）契，姜嫄踏上大人的足迹感生后稷……以及女娲抟黄土而作人等等，就都是这种女性崇拜的产物。

老子的时代，早已处于父系社会，女性的主导地位也早被男性所取代，但女性崇拜的文化因子并没有消失，它积淀在我们民族文化的深层结构和思维方式之中。老子思想中尚柔守雌、重阴尚慈、好静处下的处世态度，就明显地具有某种女性文化的特征。

老子说："我有三件持身的宝物：一件叫慈，即慈爱柔和；一件叫俭，即俭朴节省；一件叫不敢和天下人争先，即甘愿谦卑处下。"（第六十七章）老子说的"慈"、"俭"、"不敢和天下人争先"的处世态度，实际都带有某种女性色彩或母性的特征。《韩非子·八说》篇有这样的话："慈母对幼子的宠爱，没有什么能比得上。"又说："母子之间的天性，是爱；君臣之间所考虑的，则是互相算计。"可见，"慈"是天然地和"爱"结合在一起的；而最无私的爱，就是母爱。所以，"慈"可以说是女性文化的特征之一。同样，"俭"、"不敢和天下人争先"，也和女性节俭、谦卑的天性有关。而老子之所以对这些女性特征加以倡导和赞赏，应该和他思想中潜藏的女性崇拜的文化传统相关。

正因为如此，老子还对水、对虚、对静、对盈等具有阴柔或女性特征的事物都加以歌颂，加以推崇，这些都使人窥

and "fullness," among which the primitive worship of females can be vaguely seen in his thought.

3. The Consequence of Chu Culture

As the accumulation of the primitive thought and culture in the ancient times in China, Laozi's thought not only was the product of the great social changes and turmoil in the late Spring and Autumn Period, but also should be regarded as the crystallization of the local Chu culture.

It is recorded in "The Biography of Laozi and Han Fei" of the *Records of the Grand Historian* that Laozi's birthplace was Qurenli of Lixiang Town in Ku County in the state of Chu, which probably means that Laozi was a native of Chu and his thought belonged to the Chu culture.

Did Laozi's thought belong to the Chu culture? Could he really be reckoned as a thinker of Chu?

It was questioned by some people who said that Laozi was born in around 571 B.C., while the state of Chen was not destroyed by Chu until 478 B.C. How could he be regarded as a thinker of Chu since his hometown was yet not annexed when he was approximately 100 years old?

Here, the history of the states of Chen and Chu must be briefly explained.

The state of Chen was a descendant of Emperor Shun, in the east of present Henan Province and northwest of Anhui Province. In the early Western Zhou Dynasty, when granting titles and territories to dukes, King Wu of Zhou sent for Gui Man, Emperor Shun's descendant, and asked him to offer sacrifices to Emperor Shun in the Chen region. Thus, the state of Chen came into being. The first ruler of Chen was called Duke Hu.

However, Chen was a comparatively small vassal state. Particularly in the Spring and Autumn Period, when the dukes contended for dominance, the Zhou Dynasty was even reduced to a small third-class state, let alone the state of Chen. The state of Chu had been already an overlord at the time. When launching a war against Chu, the state of Wu said, "The small states, located between the Yangtze River and the Han River, which the descendants of Zhou were granted, have been conquered by Chu." ❶ As Chen was close to Chu, it had long become the latter's dependency.

见到老子思想中原始女性崇拜文化的影子。

（三）楚地文化的结晶

老子思想既是春秋末期中国大变革大动荡社会现实的产物，是中国上古原始思想文化的积淀，同时也应该看作是楚国地方文化的结晶。

司马迁在《史记》中的《老子韩非列传》中说，老子的籍贯在楚国的苦县厉乡曲仁里，意思似乎是说老子属于楚国人，老子的思想属于楚文化的一部分。

老子思想真是楚文化的一部分吗？老子本人真可以算得上是楚国的思想家吗？

有人对此提出疑问，说老子约生于公元前571年，而陈国直到公元前478年才被楚国灭亡，老子将近百岁时他的家乡都还没有被楚国吞并，怎么能算作楚国的思想家呢？

这里还得对陈、楚两国的历史稍微做些交待才行。

陈国本是虞舜后代的聚居地，在今河南省东部及安徽省西北部一带。西周初年分封诸侯时，周武王就把舜的后人妫满找来，让他在陈地奉祀帝舜，这就有了陈国。陈国的第一个国君叫陈胡公。

但是，陈国是一个比较弱小的诸侯国，特别是到了春秋时期，诸侯争霸，周朝都沦为了一个三等小国，何况陈国？楚国在当时已是一霸，吴国向楚国开战理由之一说是："周朝的子孙分封在长江、汉水之间的小国，都被楚国消灭了。" ❶ 陈国邻近楚国，所以它很早就已成了楚国的附庸国。

---

❶《史记·楚世家》。

❶ "The Biography of Chu," in the *Records of the Grand Historian*.

In 533 B.C., Confucius was 19 years old and Laozi was about 39. Seeing that another internal disturbance arise in Chen at the time, King Ling of Chu sent Prince Qiji of Chu to destroy it again. Not until had King Ping of Chu succeeded to the throne, in order to establish a good image among the other dukes, he found the grandson (who fled abroad) of Duke Dao of Chen and restored the state again. Thus, Chen lingered on for decades.

In 478 B.C., King Hui of Chu of the time was not as patient as his forefathers and finally destroyed Chen. The Chen region became a dependent county of Chu. Until this year, it had been one year since Confucius passed away and Laozi was about 93 years old.

During Laozi's life, no matter whether Chen was independent or not, it was nothing but a dependency of Chu and the independence in its politics and culture was limited. In this sense, Laozi can be regarded as either a representative of the thought and culture of Chu or a thinker of Chu.

On the other hand, if we compare Laozi's thought with that of the other thinkers or philosophers of Chu earlier than or contemporary with him, we can also see some similarities between them. Therefore, it also makes sense to say that Laozi was influenced by the thinkers of Chu.

A Taoist book, *Yuzi*, was recorded before *Laozi* in "Treatise on Literature" of the *Book of Han* by Ban Gu. Yuzi's given name was Xiong, and he was the ancestor of the state of Chu in the Western Zhou Dynasty. Yu Xiong used to be the teacher of King Wen of Zhou, who once asked him the way of governing the country. Liu Xie, a famous literary theorist of Liang of the Southern Dynasties, said in his "Speculative Writings of the Masters" of *Dragon-Carving and the Literary Mind*, "Yu Xiong knew the mighty Tao, so King Wen consulted him. His lost works and anecdotes were collected and compiled into *Yuzi*, which was earlier than the speculative writings of the other masters."

Yu Xiong was the first ancestor of the state of Chu, and *Yuzi* was the beginning of the speculative writings of the masters. However, *Yuzi* available today was not that of Ban Gu's time; instead, it was extracted by the Tang people from other books. As the former *Yuzi* contained a lot of Taoist ideas, Ban Gu classified it as "Taoist." Some of Yu Xiong's words can be simply said to be identical to those of *Laozi*. For example, by extending Yu Xiong's words, "Heaven's Gifts" of *Liezi* says,

公元前533年，孔子十九岁，老子约三十九岁。楚灵王看到当时陈国又发生了内乱，就派楚公子弃疾再次灭了陈国。楚平王即位，为了在诸侯中树立自己的良好形象，把逃到国外的陈悼公的孙子找到了，重新恢复陈国。陈国又苟延残喘了几十年。

公元前478年，当时的楚惠王已没有祖先的耐心，最终灭掉了陈国。陈国的故地，成了楚国的属县。这一年，孔子已去世一年，老子约九十三岁。

在老子的一生中，不论陈国是否独立存在，它都只是楚国的一个附庸与属国，其政治上、文化上的独立性都是有限的。从这个意义上讲，说老子是楚国思想文化的代表，或者说老子是楚国的思想家，也是可以的。

如果我们把老子的思想和比老子更早或同时代的其他楚国思想家的思想作比较，我们也可以看到两者之间的某些相近或相同之处。说老子受到了楚国思想家的某些影响，也是有道理的。

班固的《汉书·艺文志》中在著录《老子》一书的前面，还记载有一部道家的著作，叫《鬻子》。鬻子，名叫鬻熊，是西周时楚国的始祖，曾担任过周文王的老师，周文王也曾向他询问治国之道。南朝萧梁时著名的文学理论家刘勰，在他的《文心雕龙·诸子篇》中说："鬻熊懂得大道，而周文王向他咨询。鬻熊的佚文遗事，被人收集编成《鬻子》一书。诸子著作产生的开端，没有比《鬻子》更早的了。"

鬻熊是楚人建国的始祖，《鬻子》这部书是诸子之书的开端。但现在我们能见到的《鬻子》一书，已不是班固见到的《鬻子》，而是唐代人从别的书里摘录来的。原来的《鬻子》有很浓厚的道家色彩，所以班固把它归在"道家"一类中。鬻熊所讲的一些话简直可以说与《老子》如出一辙，例如《列子·天瑞》一篇中引申鬻熊的话说：

Evolution is never ending. But who can perceive the secret processes of Heaven and Earth? Thus, things that are diminished here are augmented there; things that are made whole in one place suffer loss in another. Diminution and augmentation, fullness and decay are the constant accompaniments of life and death. They alternate in continuous succession, and we are not conscious of any interval. Who is able to perceive the processes?

Yu Xiong's words are interlinked with "Tao" in *Laozi*, "reaching everywhere and in no danger (of being exhausted)" (Chapter 25), and "Being and nonbeing are two phases of existence; different and easy are two states of persistence; long and short are two degrees of distance; high and low are two ranks of eminence; echo and sound are two expressions of resonance; before and after are two orders of sequence. Things always contrast in this way" (Chapter 2). Born later than Yu Xiong, Laozi was supposed to be enlightened by him. "The Yellow Emperor" of *Liezi* also quoted Yu Xiong's words,

To become tough, one must defend himself with the soft; to become strong, one must defend himself with the weak. One is sure to become tough by accumulating the soft; one is sure to become strong by accumulating the weak. What is accumulated in the examination of things at ordinary times will help one understand the development and changes of good fortune and bad fortune.

This is consistent with the above-mentioned quotation from Chapter 2 of *Laozi*, which explains the interdependence between the two parties of contradiction. Moreover, this also contains Laozi's so-called thinking of "giving first what you want to" and the concept concerning the transformation of the two parties to the opposite.Laozi said,

Reversion is the way of Tao. (Chapter 40)
Good fortune contains bad fortune and bad fortune conceals good fortune. (Chapter 58)

Yuzi's wisdom is obviously contained in Laozi's thinking.
After Yuzi, King Zhuang of Chu and Sun Shu'ao, his Prime Minister, also seemed to have more Taoist tendencies in their words and deeds. As is recorded in "The Biography of the House of Chu" of the *Records of the Grand Historian*,

In 597 B.C., King Zhuang of Chu led the troops to besiege the state of Zheng, which was conquered three months later. Bare to the waist, the

世界运转不断，天地不停变化，谁感觉到了呢？所以世上的事物在那边有减损的，则在这边有增加；在这里有成长的，就在那边有缺失。减损与增加、成长与缺失，一边开始一边在终结，来来往往，没有人感觉到了间隙。谁感觉到了呢？

鹖子的这些话，与《老子》所说的"道""周行而不殆"（第二十五章）；"故有无相生，难易相成，长短相形，高下相倾，音声相和，前后相随。恒也"（第二章）都有相通之处。鹖子在前，老子在后。老子应该受到过鹖子的启发。《列子·黄帝篇》又曾引用鹖熊的话：

如果想要刚强，一定要用柔弱来守卫；如果想要强大，一定要用弱小来守卫。积累柔弱，一定会变得刚强；积累弱小，一定会变得强大。考察事物平时所积累的是什么，可以了解祸福发展变化的方向。

这里不仅与刚才所引《老子》第二章讲矛盾双方互相依存的关系一致，而且还包含有老子所谓"欲取姑与"的思想和关于矛盾双方各向对立面转化的观念。老子说：

反者道之动。（第四十章）

祸兮，福之所倚；福兮，祸之所伏。（第五十八章）

老子的这些思想里，明显包含有鹖子的智慧。

鹖子之后，楚庄王时庄王本人和他的宰相孙叔敖的言行，似乎也有较多的道家倾向。《史记·楚世家》记载：

公元前597年，楚庄王率军围困郑国，花了三个月时间攻下来了。郑国的国君裸着上身牵着羊出来，说："我

duke of Zheng came out with a sheep and said, "Ignorant of the Tao of heaven, I couldn't serve Your Majesty well and irritated you so much that you have come to our capital city, a remote area. This is our sin. So, now, whatever you want me to do, I will do your bidding. You may, as you please, banish me to the South Sea and grant my wife and concubines to the other dukes. But, for the sake of my forefathers, please let them continue offering sacrifices and wait upon Your Majesty. This is my biggest wish. I just spoke my mind." The officials of Chu advised that the king should not approve of him. However, King Zhuang said, "The duke is willing to enslave himself so that he can surely win the trust of his people. Then how can Zheng be annihilated!" He waved the flag personally, ordering the Chu troops to retreat 30 *li* and set camps. He finally made peace with Zheng.

In King Zhuang's words and deeds, there are at least two points which reflect his Taoist tendency. On the one hand, according to him, it was not only rare for the duke of Zheng to enslave himself and "bear the humiliation of the country," but this behavior would also inevitably gain the trust of the Zheng people. In the end, Zheng would surely turn the corner and save its state. On the other hand, King Zhuang, of his own accord, ordered his troops to retreat 30 *li* and made peace with Zheng. This reflects a kind of thinking of "quitting when one is ahead" and "humility." Laozi once repeatedly stressed that "Water flows in places others reject; in this way, it comes closest to Tao" (Chapter 8); "A strong army may face attacks; a hard tree is ready for the axe" (Chapter 76); "He who bears the humiliation of the country is worthy to be called its master; he who bears the disasters of the country is worthy to be called its ruler" (Chapter 78); "A large country should not desire dominance; a small country should not seek subservience; in this way, the purposes of each are fulfilled; consequently, it is fitting for a large country to yield" (Chapter 61). King Zhuang's thinking seemed to be reflected from these words. However, the state of Jin at the time did not follow Taoist philosophy. When launching a war against the state of Chu on the pretext of rescuing the state of Zheng, Jin was seriously defeated by Chu and driven straight to the north of the Yellow River.

Sun Shu'ao became the Prime Minister of Chu three times and lost his post three times too. When he got the position, he was not jubilant. When he lost his office, he did not show any sadness. He truly transcended worldly affairs, being at ease and comfortable. Laozi said, "He disregards palaces and luxuries along the way." The statement is seemingly about Sun Shu'ao. "Illustrating Laozi" of *Han Feizi* says,

不明天道，不能好好侍奉您，使您生气，来到我们这个边蛮的国都，这都是我们的罪过。您让我做什么，我现在一定唯命是听！把我流放到南海，把我的妻妾赏赐给诸侯，也都随您怎么办。如果您看在我祖宗的份上，不让他们断绝了祭祀，改让他们来侍奉您，这是我的最大的愿望。我对您说的都是我心里话。"楚国的大臣们都劝庄王不要同意。但庄王说："郑国国君能够甘居人下，一定可以得到人民的信任，郑国哪是别人灭得了的！"楚庄王亲自挥动旗帜，指挥楚军后退三十里安营，最终和郑国讲了和。

在楚庄王的言行中，至少有两点反映出他的道家思想倾向：一是他认为郑君能甘然处下，"受国之诟"，这不仅难得，而且他认为这种行为必然会得到郑国人民的信任，郑国一定能转危为安，保存江山社稷；二是他主动指挥楚军后退，并与郑国讲和。这反映了一种见好就收、谦卑处下的思想。老子曾反复强调水"处众之所恶，故几道"（第八章）；"兵强则灭，木强则折"（第七十六章）；"受国之诟，是谓社稷主；受国之不祥，是谓天下王。"（第七十八章）"大国不过欲兼畜人，小国不过欲入事人。夫两者各得其所欲，大者宜为下。"（第六十一章）这些地方，似乎有楚庄王思想的影子。当时晋国不以道家哲学为原则处理这件事，派大军以救郑的名义与楚军开战，结果被楚国打得大败，一直被赶到黄河北边去了。

孙叔敖曾三次担任楚国的令尹（相当于宰相），又三次失去官职，他得到令尹职位没有一点喜色，丢了官职也没有忧色。真是超然物外，晏然自处。老子说："虽有荣观，燕处超然。"说的好像就是他这个人。《韩非子·喻老篇》说：

After defeating the Jin army at Bi, King Zhuang of Chu led his troops to the north of the Yellow River. After returning in triumph, he granted Sun Shu'ao territories, but Sun Shu'ao only asked for the land near the Han River, a territory covered with gravel. Later, the state of Chu granted the law, which stipulated that the next generation of the paid ministers should turn in their fiefs. Only Sun Shu'ao's fief was saved. The reason was that the land was so infertile that his many generations possessed the fief. Therefore, the statement that "He whose faith is rooted in Tao will never waver; he whose action is guided by Tao will never slip" is actually about such a person as Sun Shu'ao.

Sun Shu'ao's behavior is what was summarized in "The World of Man" of *Huainanzi*: "Things gain by losing." Han Fei referred to Laozi's statement that "He whose faith is rooted in Tao will never waver; he whose action is guided by Tao will never slip" as the summary of Sun Shu'ao's behavior. However, this probably neither conforms to the fact, nor can it reveal the deep connotation contained in his behavior—Sun Shu'ao "gained by losing" just because he "flowed in places the others rejected" like water. It is stated in Chapter 7 of *Laozi*, "Therefore, the sage withdraws but still shines forth; he denies himself and thus is saved. Is it not because of his selflessness that he has attained his purposes?" Laozi definitely absorbed the historical experience, thought and wisdom of the state of Chu into his works, so he was regarded as a thinker of Chu in the Warring States Period by the posterity.

Laozi is also known as *Tao Te Ching*. Taoists were also called "moralists"

　　楚庄王在邲地打败晋国军队之后，把楚军开到了黄河北边，凯旋之后封赏宰相孙叔敖。孙叔敖请求汉水附近的土地，布满沙石的地方。楚国后来颁布法令，享受奉禄的大臣到第二代就要收回封地，只有孙叔敖受封的那块土地保存下来了。这块地不被楚国收回的原因，是因为那是块贫瘠的土地，所以孙叔敖好多代都享有这块封地。所以说："善于树立的拔不掉，善于抱持的脱不开，子孙后代因此世世祭祀不中断"说的就是孙叔敖这样的人。

　　孙叔敖的行为，《淮南子·人间训》概括为"损之而益"。韩非把老子的"善建者不拔，善抱者不脱，子孙以其祭祀世世不辍"的话，说成好像是对孙叔敖行为的概括。但这既可能不符合事实，也似乎尚未能准确揭示出孙氏行为所包含的深刻含义——孙叔敖是因为像水那样"处众人之所恶"，才实现"损之而益"的。《老子》第七章说："是以圣人后其身而身先，外其身而身存。非以其无私邪？故能成其私。"老子应该是把楚国的这些历史经验和思想智慧吸收到自己的著作中去了，后人才把老子视为战国楚国的思想家的。

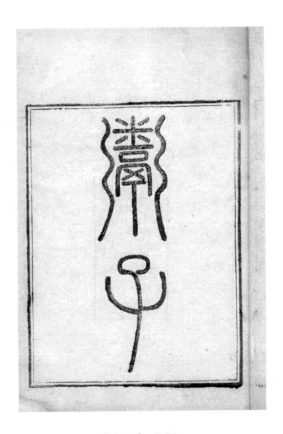

《鹖子》书影

Picture of *Yuzi*

四 尊道而贵德——老子的道论和德论

Chapter IV　Respecting Tao and Honoring Virtue
　　　　　　　——Laozi's Theory of Tao and Virtue

in the Han Dynasty. In "The Biography of Laozi and Han Fei," Sima Qian referred to Laozi's book as "explaining Tao and virtue in 5 000 Chinese characters." Chapter 51 of *Laozi* says,

Tao gives birth to everything and virtue nurtures all things; existence takes shape and things are completed. All things respect Tao and honor virtue.

Judging from this statement, "Tao" and "virtue" are indeed the core concept of Laozi's thought, and play a key role in his ideological system.

1. What Is Tao?

The Chinese character "Tao" appeared in the inscriptions on the ancient bronze objects as early as the beginning of the Zhou Dynasty. It originally referred to the way for walking. During hundreds of years from the Western Zhou Dynasty to the Spring and Autumn Period, the meaning of "Tao" gradually became abstract. In the beginning, it denoted some specific claims, principles and methods that evolved into the abstract laws, principles and methods, and then, the categories, such as "the Tao of heaven" and "the Tao of man," were formed.

Laozi's theory of Tao was a theoretical innovation based on his assimilation of the experience and outcomes of predecessors' thinking. He not only elevated "Tao" to the level of cosmology and the origin of all things, but also regarded it as the "Tao" of the origin of the universe. Together with "the ancient Tao," "the Tao of heaven," "the Tao of man" and "the way of long life and eternal vision," which were all summarized from natural phenomena and human lives, the "Tao of the origin of the universe" constituted a complete theoretical system. The Taoist school in ancient China was thus established.

What is Laozi's "Tao" on earth? How are we to interpret the connotation of his theory of Tao? In history, people who annotated *Laozi* differed greatly on these questions. Heshanggong's *Commentaries on Laozi* in the Western Han Dynasty believed that "Tao" was actually *yuan qi*—vital breath in the original state. Heshanggong said, "Coming from nothingness, inhaling and exhaling the breath and pursuing enlightenment are the origin of heaven and earth." ❶ Later, this viewpoint was adopted by scholars of *Laozi*, who had the materialist tendency. The explanation of Wang Bi in the Wei and Jin dynasties exerted the greatest influence. He said, "Tao produces and comletes all things with the

《老子》一书，又称《道德经》。道家在汉代也被称为"道德家"，司马迁在《老子韩非列传》中，即称老子著书为"述道德之意五千言。"《老子》第五十一章说：

> 道生之，德畜之，物形之，器（势）成之。是以万物莫不尊道而贵德。

由老子的这段话我们可以看出，"道"和"德"的确是老子思想中的核心概念，在老子的思想体系中占有极其重要地位。

（一）道是什么

"道"这个字最早出现于周初的金文中，本义指人行走的道路。从西周到春秋的数百年间，"道"的意义逐渐抽象化，先是表示一些较具体的主张、原则、方法，然后演变为抽象的规律、原则、方法，并形成了"天之道"（或"天道"）、"人之道"（或"人道"）等范畴。

老子的道论，是他在吸收前人思维经验与成果的基础上的理论创新。他不仅将"道"上升到宇宙发生论的高度，而且还将这个作为宇宙总根源的"道"，和从各种自然现象与人类生活中概括出来的"古之道"、"天之道"、"人之道"、"长生久视之道"等等，组成了一个完整的理论体系，创建了中国古代的道家学派。

老子的"道"到底是什么？我们应该怎样理解老子道论的内涵？历史上解释《老子》的人对此分歧很大。西汉河上公的《老子注》认为，"道"实际是一种原始状态的气——元气。他说：道"吐气布化，出于虚无，为天地本始也。"[1]后来具有唯物主义倾向的《老子》学者多采用这种看法。魏晋时期的王

---

[1]《老子河上公注》第一章。

[1] Chapter 1 of *Commentaries on Laozi by Heshanggong*.

formless and nameless." Tao is known as non-being. All things are linked and produced by nonbeing, which is named "Tao." Tao exists formlessly in tranquility and it cannot become visible, thus it is "nonbeing." ❶

Sima Guang, a historian of the Northern Song Dynasty, wrote a book entitled *True Classic of the Way and the Power*. Explaining the statement that "Tao can be defined as 'Tao,' but it is not the eternal 'Tao' " of *Laozi*, he said, "When ordinary people are talking about 'Tao,' they always say that Tao as reality is subtle and cannot be explained in words. But, Laozi's theory of Tao is not like that. According to him, Tao can be defined as 'Tao,' but it is not the eternal 'Tao.' " Different from other explanations, Sima Guang's interpretation was a roundabout way, which focused on the explanation of "Tao" from the perspective of discourse on " Tao."

Nowadays, the so-called "materialism" and "idealism" are the most controversial concepts about Laozi's "Tao." One view is that his "Tao" is an objective "natural way" and it is "materialistic," while the other view is that his "Tao" is the existence of *a priori* spirit, which is " idealistic."

Throughout *Laozi*, "Tao" is mentioned in more than 30 chapters, in most of which the concept of "Tao" is directly quoted, while in some other chapters, "Tao" is modified, such as "the eternal Tao" in "Tao can be defined as 'Tao,' but it is not the eternal 'Tao' " of Chapter 1; "the ancient Tao" in "Govern your country with the ancient Tao, and you will know the origin of all things" of Chapter 14; "the mighty Tao" in "When the mighty Tao is discarded, humaneness and righteousness arise" of Chapter 18; "the Tao of heaven" in "To retire after success is the Tao of heaven" of Chapter 9; "the way of long life and eternal vision" in "This is called 'deep-rootedness,' the way of long life and eternal vision" of Chapter 59; "the Tao of heaven" in "The Tao of heaven is like the stretching of an archer's bow" and "the Tao of man" in "Man takes from those who have much less" of Chapter 77.

This indicates that Tao possesses multi-level connotations in Laozi's theory of Tao. The highest category is "the mighty Tao" and "the eternal Tao," namely, the origin and the general law of all things. Next to it are " the Tao of heaven" that functions as the natural law and "the Tao of man," which is the law of human society. "The ancient Tao," "the Tao of governing a country,"

弼的解释影响最大，他说："道以无形无名成济万物。" ❶ 即是说，道无形无名，但却生出了万物，养育形成了万物。

北宋的历史学家司马光写了一本《道德真经论》，他借解释《老子》中的"道可道，非常道"说："世俗的人们谈论道时，都说道体微妙，不能用言语来解说，但老子的道论却不是这样。老子是说道也是可道的，但不是一般人所说的道。"这种看法，侧重从人对"道"的言说角度来解释"道"，这是一种迂回的解释方式，与一般人的解释不同。

现代以来，对老子"道"概念争议最多的，是所谓"唯物"与"唯心"的问题。一种观点认为老子的"道"是客观存在的"自然之道"，是"唯物主义"的；另一种看法则认为，老子的"道"是先验的精神存在，是"唯心主义"的。

在《老子》一书中，共有三十多章言及"道"，大多数章中直接用"道"概念，但在有些章节中，又对"道"加限定。如《老子》第一章中"道可道，非常（恒）道"中的"常（恒）道"，第十四章"执古之道，以御今之有"中的"古之道"，第十八章"大道废，有仁义"中的"大道"，第九章"功成身遂，天之道"中的"天之道"，第五十九章"是谓深根固柢，长生久视之道"中的"长生久视之道"，第七十七章"天之道其犹张弓"和"人之道则不然"中的"天之道"、"人之道"等等。

这说明，在老子的道论中，"道"具有多层次的内涵。作为"大道"、"恒道"，即世界万物产生的总根源和总规律的"道"，是最高层次的范畴。其次，则是作为自然规律的"天之道"和作为人类社会规律的"人之道"。而作为人类社会规律的"人之道"，又有所谓"古之道"、"治国之道"、"人伦之道"、"长生久

❶ 王弼：《老子注》第二十八章。

❶ Chapter 28 of *Commentaries on Laozi* by Wang Bi.

"the Tao of human relations" and "the way of long life and eternal vision" also belong to "the Tao of man." Chapter 1 of *Laozi* says, "Tao can be defined as 'Tao,' but it is not the eternal 'Tao.' " The first Chinese character "Tao" is a noun, acting as the highest category of his philosophy, which is the origin and general law of all things. As this "Tao" is absolute and eternal, Laozi also referred to it as "the eternal Tao." The second "Tao" is a verb, which means "can be defined." It is self-evident that at the beginning of *Laozi*, "Tao" is divided into the specific "Tao" that can be defined (such as the Tao of human relations and the Tao of governing a country) and the "Tao" that cannot be defined—"the mighty Tao" or "the eternal Tao."

According to Laozi, it is because "Tao," the highest category of philosophy, has features beyond the ordinary "Tao" that it should be called "the eternal Tao" and "the mighty Tao."

The significance of its metaphysical ontology is supposed to be the first feature of "Tao." "The Great Treatise I" of the *Book of Changes* says, "That which is antecedent to the material form exists, we say, as Tao, and that which is subsequent to the material form exists, we say, as a definite substance." Entity is also known as the root or the origin in Chinese philosophy. Chapter 25 of *Laozi* says,

> A formless entity existed prior to heaven and earth. Silent and void, it stands alone and unchanging, and can be considered as the mother of all things under heaven. Not knowing its name, I call it "Tao"; perhaps I should call it " greatness."

Here, apriority of "Tao" and the metaphysical transcendence of "Tao" are both emphasized. The reason why "Tao" is regarded as *a priori* is that "Tao" existed prior to heaven and earth and it is the mother of all things. "Tao" is said to be the metaphysical transcendence because it is silent, void, formless and even nameless. *Laozi* says, "Names can be used for its name, but they do not give the eternal name" (Chapter 1); and "Tao is eternal and nameless" (Chapter 32 and 37). That which can be named is a kind of specific and limited existence. As "Tao" is nameless, it is metaphysical and transcendent. We are forced to call it "Tao" because there are no other options. We are forced to call it "greatness"; moreover, we usually call it accurately "the mighty Tao" and

视之道"等等。《老子》第一章说："道可道，非常（恒）道。"第一个"道"字是名词，是指作为他的哲学最高范畴的"道"，即世界万物的总根源、总规律。这个"道"是绝对的和永恒的，所以他又称之为"常道"（"常"字，帛书甲、乙本皆作"恒"，汉代为避汉文帝刘恒的名讳而改）。第二个"道"字则是动词，是言说的意思。可见《老子》一开头就是把"道"分为"可道"的具体的"道"（如各种人伦之道、治国理政之道）和不可言说的"道"——"大道"或"常（恒）道"的。

老子认为，作为最高哲学范畴的"道"，之所以应该叫作"常（恒）道"、"大道"，是因为它具有超出一般"道"的特点。

老子之"道"的第一个特点，应该是它的形而上的本体论的意义。《周易·系辞上》说："形而上者谓之道，形而下者谓之器。"意思是说，没有具体形态的虚无之物，就叫作"道"；有形体可见知的物体，就叫作"器"。本体，在中国哲学中又称为本根、本源。《老子》第二十五章说：

> 有物混成，先天地生。寂兮寥兮，独立而不改，周行而不殆，可以为天下母。吾不知其名，强字之曰道，强为之名曰大。

这段话既强调了"道"的先验性，也强调了"道"的形上超越性。说"道"先验，因为它在天地产生之前就已存在，它是天下万物之母；说它形上超越，因为它空虚寂寥，没有任何具体的形象，甚至连名字都没有。《老子》说："名可名，非常名"（第一章）；又说："道恒无名"（第三十二章、第三十七章）。能叫出名字的，是一种具体的、有限的存在。"道"连名字也没有，所以它是真正形而上的和超越的。"道"这个名字也是我们在没有办法的情况下，勉强给它安上去的。我们勉强称它为"大"，而且还常常以我们人类的准确说法把它叫作

"the eternal Tao." But, in fact, it is with reluctance that we name it "Tao" ; let alone "the mighty Tao" or "the eternal Tao." Therefore, usually Laozi only used the name "Tao" to call it.

Though "Tao" is so void, formless, metaphysical and transcendent, it does not mean that it exists in void, or does not exist at all. It is an absolutely genuine "substance." Chapter 21 of *Laozi* says,

> Tao is opaque and obscure. Opaque and obscure, yet it has an image within; obscure and opaque, yet it has substance within. Dim and dark, yet it has a spirit within, which is genuine and filled with truth.

In many other places of the book, Laozi also repeatedly mentioned the feature of the metaphysical ontology of "Tao," the *a priori*, formless, nameless feature of real existence. For example, Chapter 4 of *Laozi* says, Tao is a void that never drains with use; it is an abyss from that all things spring. It blunts its sharpness and untangles its knots; it conceals its brilliance and is as humble as dust; it appears to exist like a visible void. I do not know how it was conceived; it appears to have preceded the heavenly gods. Chapter 14 says,

> What we look at but do not see is called "invisible" ; what we listen to but do not hear is called "inaudible" ; what we reach for but do not grasp is called "intangible." These three are indefinable; as a result, they merge into oneness. As for oneness, its other name is Tao, its top does not seem opaque, its bottom does not seem obscure. Indescribably immense, it returns to nothingness. It is called "opaque obscurity."

Perhaps, his so-called "Tao" cannot be clearly explained by the original Chinese theories. Shi Sengzhao of the late Eastern Jin Dynasty incorporated "Tao" with "tathata" in Buddhism, saying that the characteristic of "Tao" was "neither existent nor non-existent, both existent and non-existent." His explanation was highly thought of.

The second feature of "Tao" is that it has the significance of cosmogony. The so-called cosmogony refers to the mother-child relationship between "Tao" and all things. Formless and nameless, "Tao" is not anything specific, nor does it have nothing to do with all things. Laozi once said that "Tao" was the root of everything, from which came all things. If summarized in philosophical language, it is what Chapter 1 says,

"大道"、"常（恒）道"。不过，老子通常只用"道"这个名字称呼它。

尽管"道"是如此空虚无形而形上超越，但这并不意味着它是虚幻的存在，更不是不存在。它是绝对真实的存在"物"。《老子》第二十一章说：

> 道之为物，惟恍惟惚。惚兮恍兮，其中有象；恍兮惚兮，其中有物。窈兮冥兮，其中有精；其精甚真，其中有信。

老子在其他很多地方也曾反复提到"道"的这种形而上的本体论特点，即先验的、无形无名而真实存在的品性。《老子》第四章说，"道"虽然如器虚中无物，但却容纳万物而不可满盈，它好像无形无物，却无时无处不有。我不知道它什么时候产生，大概在天帝之前就已出现。第十四章又说：

> 视之不见名曰夷，听之不闻名曰希，搏之不得名曰微。此三者不可致诘，故混而为一。其上不皦，其下不昧，绳绳不可名，复归于无物。是谓无状之状，无物之象，是谓惚恍。

也许老子的所谓"道"，用中国原有的理论都无法说清，东晋末年的释僧肇就把"道"和佛教的"真如"混同起来，说"道"的这个特点是"非有非无，亦有亦无"。大家都非常佩服僧肇的解释。

老子"道"的第二个特点，是它同时具有宇宙生成论的意义。所谓宇宙生成论，是就"道"与万物的母子关系来说的。"道"无形无名，不是任何具体的事物，但它却不是与世界的万事万物无关的。老子曾说道是天地万物的根本，天地万物都是从那里面生出来的。这个意思用哲学的语言来概括，就是《老子》第一章所说的：

The nameless Tao is the origin of all things; the named Tao is the mother of all things.

"Tao" is oneness of being and nonbeing, while "origin" equals to "mother" in meaning, which claims "Tao" to be the mother of all things.

In fact, Laozi already said that "Tao" was formless and nameless, and that even the designation of Tao was given "with reluctance." So how can it be said to be oneness of being and nonbeing? The reason is that in the following chapters Laozi also said, "The 'named' and 'nameless' designate the same Tao; from mystery to mystery leads this gateway to all wonders." This tells us that being and nonbeing are products of "Tao," and "Tao" is not the simple addition of the two. "Tao" is initially invisible, so being and nonbeing coming from it are also invisible and mysterious, which become the more direct source of all things. We think that in Chapter 1 of *Laozi*, the "nameless" refers to "Tao" and the "named" should be "oneness" of being and nonbeing. Chapter 42 of *Laozi* says,

From Tao comes oneness; from oneness comes the duality of *yin* and *yang*; from duality comes the equilibrium of *yin* and *yang*; from equilibrium comes all things under heaven. All things embody *yin* and *yang* as opposing parts; the blending of both brings equilibrium.

Throughout history, people have had different interpretations about the meaning of "oneness" in the above passage. We hold the view that if "Tao" is regarded as the nameless and more original root or entity, "metaphysics" of being and nonbeing is viewed as "oneness," and "duality" is considered as *yin* and *yang* embodied in all things as opposing parts, then the conversion process from ontology to cosmogony in Laozi's thought can be seen clearly and his pattern of cosmogony will become very explicit—"Tao" (the real entity that cannot be defined) → "oneness" (the unification of being and nonbeing) → "duality" (*yin* and *yang*) → "equilibrium" (heaven, earth and man) → "all wonders" (all things).

If summed up most concisely in Laozi's words, the pattern is what he said in Chapter 40,

All things are born from some being, which is born from the nonbeing of Tao.

Chapter 34 says, "Tao is everywhere, flowing left and right; it claims for itself no success or achievements." Chapter 39 reads, "Since ancient times, things have been endowed with Tao; heaven has thus been clarified; earth has thus been stabilized; gods have thus been deified; valleys have thus been

无名，天地之始；有名，万物之母。

"道"是有、无的统一体，"始"和"母"都是一个意思，都是说"道"是万物的母体。

其实，老子早就说过"道"是无形无名的，连名字都只是"强为之名"的结果，怎么能把它说成有、无的统一体呢？因为下文老子又说："此二者同出而异名，同谓之玄，玄之又玄，众妙之门。"这就是告诉人们，有、无都是"道"的产物，而不是说"道"等于有、无的相加。"道"本来是幽深隐微的，所以它生出来的有、无也是幽微难明的；而迷雾重重的有、无，又成了天地万物更直接的源头。所以我们认为《老子》第一章的"无名"、"有名"应该连读："无名"指"道"，"有名"应该是有、无相结合的"一"。《老子》第四十二章说：

道生一，一生二，二生三，三生万物。万物负阴而抱
阳，冲气以为和。

这段话中的"一"是什么，历来的解释也不同。我们认为，如果把"道"当成不可名状的、更原始的本根或本体，把有、无的"玄同"当作"一"，把"二"当成万物所"负"、"抱"的阴阳二气，则老子思想中由本体论到宇宙生成论的转换过程既可以看清，他的宇宙生成论的模式也就变得十分明晰了：道（人不可言说的真实本体）→"一"（有、无的统一体）→"二"（阴、阳二气）→"三"（天、地、人）→"众妙"（万物）。

老子的这一宇宙生成论的模式，如果用他自己的话作最简要的概括，就是《老子》第四十章所说的：

天下万物生于有，有生于无。

《老子》第三十四章说："大道氾（泛）兮，其可左右：万物恃之以生而不辞。"第三十九章也说："天得一以清，地得一以宁，神得一以灵，谷得一以盈，万物得一以生。"这些地方

vitalized." These statements show that things do not come directly from "Tao," which is only the basis for the existence of all things; "Tao" can only generate "oneness," then "oneness" generates "duality" and "duality" produces "equilibrium." "Oneness," "duality" and "equilibrium" are already concrete designations, that is, "the named" ; hence it is said that all things are born from some being (the named). However, the named "being" is born from " the nameless" — "Tao." So, it is said that being is born from nonbeing of Tao. The same meaning can be seen in the statement that "Tao is the concern of all things under heaven" (Chapter 64).

The third feature of "Tao" is the so-called "Tao patterning itself after its own nature." Chapter 25 says,

> Tao is great; heaven is great; earth is great; the king is great. Among the four "great" in the universe, the king is only one of them. Man patterns himself after earth; earth patterns itself after heaven; heaven patterns itself after Tao; Tao patterns itself after its own nature.

The statement that "Tao is great; heaven is great; earth is great; the king is great" is different from that of the Bamboo-slip *Laozi*, which goes like this, "Heaven is great; earth is great; Tao is great; the king is great." People annotating the Bamboo-slip *Laozi* were of the opinion that "Tao" on the bamboo slips referred to "the Tao of man." Here, however, the statement that "Tao patterns itself after its own nature" is about the characteristics of "the eternal Tao" or "the mighty Tao." So, it is rather preferable to adopt the sentence order of the current *Laozi*. Then, what is "patterning itself after its own nature" ? The "nature" is not only the natural world but also the laws of nature, that is, the so-called "doing nothing" and "being natural." Wang Bi's *Commentaries on Laozi* says, "That which patterns after its own nature patterns itself after square when the nature is square and after circle when the nature is circular. This is not resistant to the nature." Simply speaking, "patterning itself after its own nature" means complying with the laws of things, namely, "doing nothing," rather than making too much interference. Chapter 17 says,

> Thus, when his work is done, his aim achieved; all the people will say, "We did it ourselves."

Chapter 64 also says,

> He helps everything to stay its natural way and constantly refrains from any interference.

The "natural way," here, refers to "Tao." Since "Tao" is the highest existence, why does it have to comply with and pattern itself after the nature?

都表明天地万物不是直接从"道"产生的,"道"只是万物存在的根据,"道"只能产生"一",然后"一"生"二","二"生"三"。"一"、"二"、"三"都已是一个个具体的名称,即"有名",故曰"天下万物生于有(名)";而这些有名字的"有",又都生于"无名"的"道"。故曰"有生于无。"《老子》第六十四章说:"道者,万物之奥(蕴藏)。"说的也是这个意思。

老子"道"的第三个特点,是所谓"道法自然"。《老子》第二十五章说:

道大,天大,地大,王亦大。域中有四大,而王居其一焉。人法地,地法天,天法道,道法自然。

这段话中的"道大,天大,地大,王亦大",楚简《老子》作"天大,地大,道大,王亦大。"注释楚简《老子》的人,都认为简文中的"道"是指"人道"。但是,我们这里说的"道法自然",是讲的"常(恒)道"或"大道"的特点。所以,这几句话还是依通行本《老子》的语句顺序为好。什么叫效法自然呢?这个"自然",既是指自然界,更是指自然的法则,即所谓"无为"、"自然而然"。王弼《老子注》说:"法自然者,在方而法方,在圆而法圆,于自然无所违也。"简单地说,"法自然"就是做任何事情时,都不要对事物作多的干预,而应该顺应事物自己的规律,就是要"无为"。《老子》第十七章说:

功成事遂,百姓皆谓我自然。

第六十四章又说:

以辅万物之自然,而不敢为。

这里的"自然",都是指"道"而言的。"道"已经是最高的存在了,它为什么还要遵循和效法自然呢?这是因为"道"

The reason is that "Tao" determines its own existence and movement according to its own conditions, while this in itself is the natural way, complying with or demonstrating the natural laws. Meanwhile, for all things, "Tao" "gives birth without possessing, works without taking credit and guides without dominating" (Chapter 51). This state, in terms of "Tao," is that "the Tao in its regular course does nothing," while in terms of all things, is that "they naturally flourish." Thus, it is said, "Tao patterns itself after its own nature."

2. What Is Virtue?

The Chinese character "virtue" (*Te*) can be found on many oracle bone inscriptions and it was supposed to indicate that the road was very straight. However, this was nothing but a guess. According to the convincing documents, by the early Western Zhou Dynasty, "virtue" was already close in meaning to that of modern Chinese, namely, morality or virtue. *Greater Odes* of the *Book of Poetry* has a poem entitled "Zheng Min," which says, "Heaven, in giving birth to the multitudes of the people, to every faculty and relationship, annexed its law. The people possess this normal nature, and they consequently love its normal virtue." "Announcement of the Duke of Shao" of the *Classic of History* says, "Let the king sedulously cultivate the virtue of reverence." Kong Yingda of the Tang Dynasty put the sentence this way, "This requests King Cheng of Zhou to immediately show respect for the virtuous." It is obvious that "virtue" had the concept of morality and virtue already.

In the works of the early Western Zhou Dynasty, there were many cases of the frequent uses of the concept of "virtue." These concepts of "virtue" all referred to the virtue of people, the good virtue. "Charge to Zhong of Cai" of the *Classic of History* says, "Great Heaven has no partial affections; it helps only the virtuous." Chapter 79 of *Laozi* says, "The Tao of heaven is impartial; it always upholds men of virtue," which should be a quotation from of the *Classic of History*. According to *Zuo Zhuan*, in the third year (588 B.C.) of Duke Cheng of Jin, when, Zhi Ying, a Jin prisoner of war, was released, the king of Chu asked how Zhi Ying would repay him after returning home. Zhi Ying replied, "I don't have any bitterness and Your Majesty did not do me any favor, either. Without any bitterness or favor, I don't know there is any sense in repaying." Chapter 63 of *Laozi* says, "Take small favors as great ones and few favors as many; reward bitterness with virtue." It is obvious that Laozi's idea

以它自己的状况为依据或原因来决定自己的存在和运动，这本身就是一种自然而然的表现，符合或表现着自然的法则。同时，"道"对万物是"生而不有，为而不恃，长而不宰"的（第五十一章）。这种状态从"道"这一方面来看，是"道常无为"；从万物这一方面来看，就是"莫之命而常自然。"所以说，"道法自然。"

（二）德是什么

"德"字在甲骨文中已有很多用例，表示道路很直的意思。不过，这只是一种推测，不能说得十分肯定。根据可信的文献记载，到西周初年时，"德"字已经和现代汉语"德"的语义相近，即道德或品德的意思。《诗经》的《大雅》中有《烝民》一诗说："天生民烝，有物有则，民之秉彝，好是懿德。"《尚书》中《召诰》篇说："王其疾敬德。"唐代孔颖达对这一句的解释是："这是叫周成王马上崇敬有道德的人。"可见，那时的"德"概念，已都是道德、品德的意思。

西周初期的著作里，就已经很频繁地使用"德"概念。这些"德"概念都是指人的德行、品德，而且是美好的品德。《尚书·蔡仲之命》说："皇天无亲，惟德是辅。"意思是说，皇天是公正无私的，它只帮助和保佑那些有道德的人。《老子》第七十九章说："天道无亲，常与善人。"在这里老子应该是引用了《尚书》"皇天无亲，惟德是辅"的大意。《左传》记载，成公三年（公元前588年），楚国释放晋国的战俘知罃时，楚王曾问知罃，回国后用什么来报答我。知罃回答说："我没有什么可怨恨的，楚王您对我也没有什么恩德。既没有怨恨，也没有恩德，我不知道有什么好报答的。"《老子》第六十三章说："大小多少，报怨以德。"显然，老子的这种观念，与他出生之

can be traced to the same origin with the concepts of "rewarding bitterness" and "rewarding virtue" existing before his birth. The difference is that Laozi did not entirely accept the concepts; instead, he found a feasible way, that is, "rewarding bitterness with virtue," with a view of resolving the endless human disputes.

Throughout *Laozi*, "virtue" is mentioned in 14 chapters, the number of which is obviously less than that of chapters involving "Tao." This is probably one of the reasons that *Laozi* is called *Tao Te Ching* rather than *Te Tao Ching* by the posterity. In spite of this, the concept of "virtue" is still important, second to the concept of "Tao" in the book.

Then, what is the so-called "virtue" ? The definition was not directly given in the book. Explanations of its concept were made by the posterity in accordance with the diction in the book.

In ancient China, Han Fei was the first person to explain the concept of "virtue." In explaining the statement that "a man of superior virtue cares not for superficial virtue, and so he is virtuous" (Chapter 38), "Explaining Laozi" of *Han Feizi* says,

> "Virtue" is internal. Acquirement is external. The mind of a man of superior virtue does not indulge in external things. If the mind does not indulge in external things, the personality will become perfect. The personality that is perfect is called "virtue." In other words, "virtue" is the acquirement of the personality.

Wang Bi of the Wei and Jin dynasties also explained this statement in his *Commentaries on Laozi*. He said,

> "Virtue" is acquirement. It can always be kept without being lost, beneficial without being damaged, so "virtue" acts as its name. Where can "virtue" be acquired? It can be acquired from "Tao." How can "virtue" be fully shown? The role of "nonbeing" must be fully played, and then all things will not be formless.

It should be said that both explanations about the concept of "virtue" grasped some features of Laozi's theory of "virtue." For example, Han Fei said, "'Virtue' is the internal personality." Wang Bi said, "'Virtue' is acquirement." Both of them precisely grasped the stipulation that "virtue" was the intrinsic

前就原已有之的"报怨"、"报德"观是一脉相承的。不同的只是，老子不是全盘地接受了原有的"以怨报怨，以德报德"的观念，而是为化解人类没完没了的怨怨相报的纷争，指出了一条可行之路，即"以德报怨"。

在《老子》一书中，讨论到"德"的地方，总共有十四章。这个数量，明显要少于涉及"道"的部分。这也可能是《老子》一书后来被称为《道德经》而不称为《德道经》的一个原因吧。尽管如此，"德"仍是《老子》中最重要的概念，是《老子》中地位仅次于"道"的概念。

那么，老子的所谓"德"又是指什么呢？《老子》书中并没有直接的界说，后人根据《老子》一书的文辞对"德"概念做出了解释。

在中国古代最早对老子的"德"概念作出解释的人，是韩非。《韩非子·解老》解释《老子》第三十八章"上德不德，是以有德"时说：

"德"，是事物内部具有的；得，是事物从外部得到的。具有"上德"的人精神不游离于自身之外。精神不游离于外，自身内在的本质就保全了。自身内在的本质就叫"德"。"德"是得之于自身的。

魏晋的王弼的《老子注》对这两句话也有解释，他说：

"德"就是"得"的意思。总能保持得而不失，有利而没有损害，所以就用"德"来作为它的名字。从哪里得到"德"呢？从"道"那儿得到的。怎么才能完全表现出"德"呢？充分发挥"无"的作用，万物就没有不能形成的。

韩非、王弼对老子"德"概念的解说，应该说都抓住了老子"德"论的一些特征。如韩非说："德是事物内在的本质。"王弼说："德是得的意思。"他们都准确抓住了"德"为事物内

endowment and personality of things, while the stipulation was derived from the features of "Tao." In terms of "virtue" covered in *Laozi*, it might be said that the theory of "virtue" mainly includes the following features:

Firstly, seen from the relationship among "Tao," "virtue" and things, "virtue" comes from "Tao" and is inherent within things. Chapter 51 of *Laozi* says, "Tao gives birth to and virtue nurtures all things; existence takes shape and things are completed. All things respect Tao and honor virtue." This statement already shows the relationship among "Tao," "virtue" and things. On the one hand, in terms of the relationship between "Tao" and "virtue," "virtue" is next to "Tao" in importance, it is the embodiment of "Tao," and it represents "Tao." Therefore, Chapter 21 says, "A man of superior virtue follows Tao alone." On the other hand, seen from the relationship between "virtue" and all things, "virtue" is the "Tao" inherent within all things, and it is the nature of all things. So, "virtue" nurtures all things while all things "respect Tao and honor virtue." The relationship between "virtue" and all things is shown by the statement in Chapter 51, "Tao gives birth to and nurtures all things; it guides and gives vitality; it fosters fruition and maturity; it feeds and shelters everything." Therefore, the "virtue" of giving birth without possessing is held in high esteem by all things.

In fact, the pre-Qin Taoists later than Laozi, such as Zhuangzi and Guanzi gave many explanations of the features of the meaning of "virtue," which were also done in terms of the relationship between "Tao" and "virtue" and the relationship between "virtue" and "things." Zhuangzi said, "If there were not the Tao, the bodily form would not have life, and its life, without the virtue, would not be manifested," and "From all things could be produced is what we call virtue." ❶ It can be seen that his opinion is the same as that of Han Fei and Wang Bi. *Guanzi* said, "The void and formless is named Tao. That which nurtures all things is 'virtue,' " and " 'Virtue' is the shelter of Tao, from which all things could be produced. Therefore, virtue means acquirement, which explains the way it is." ❷ His opinion is also identical with that of Laozi and his junior scholars.

Laozi's theory of "virtue" has some opinions similar to Confucians, and their opinions are even interlinked. Confucians said, "Heaven, in giving birth to the multitudes of the people, to every faculty and relationship annexed its

在禀赋、内在质的规定性，而这种规定性又得之于"道"的特征。综合《老子》中的"德"论部分，我们可以说老子的"德"论主要包括如下特点：

首先，从"德"与"道"和事物的关系来看，"德"是得自于"道"而内在于事物的。《老子》第五十一章说："道生之，德畜之，物形之，器（势）成之。是以万物莫不尊道而贵德。"这里说明了"道"、"德"、"物"之间的关系。一方面，从"德"与"道"的关系来看，"德"是"道"的下落，是"道"的化身，它代表着"道"，所以《老子》第二十一章说："孔德之容，惟道是从。"另一方面，从"德"与万物的关系来说，"德"是内在于万物中的"道"，是万物得以成为万物的本质，所以它畜养着、充实着万物；而万物则"尊道而贵德"。《老子》第五十一章用"道生之，德畜之，长之，育之，亭之，毒之，养之，覆之"，来说明"德"与万物的关系。因此万物都推崇这种施与却不自恃有功的"德"。

老子这种从"道"、"德"关系和"德"、"物"关系来说明"德"的涵义的特点，老子之后的先秦道家人物，如庄子、管子也有很多申述。庄子说："形非道不生，生非德不明。"又说："物得以生谓之德。"❶由此可以看出，这是和韩非、王弼的看法一致的。《管子》也说："虚而无形谓之道，化育万物谓之德。"又说："德者，道之舍，物得以生 故德者得也。得也者，谓其所以得然也。"❷这种观点与老子及其后学也是相同的。

老子的"德"论，甚至和儒家的观点也有某些近似之处，甚至可以说是相通的。儒家说："天生烝民，有物有则。"又说：

---

❶《庄子·天地》。
❷《管子·心术上》。

❶ "Heaven and Earth," *Zhuangzi*.
❷ "Xin Shu," *Guanzi*.

law," and "What heaven confers is called '*Xing*' (nature).' " ❶ It is identical with Laozi's statement that "Tao gives birth to and virtue nurtures all things." What is different is that Laozi referred to the intrinsic nature as "virtue," while Confucians called it "*Xing*" (nature). "Virtue" in the Taoist School refers to the essence of all things, while "*Xing*" (nature) of Confucians mainly refers to the virtue of man.

Next, the second feature of Laozi's theory is that the so-called "virtue" is also a multi-level concept with different connotations. Chapter 21 of *Laozi* says, "A man of superior virtue follows Tao alone." In Chapter 28 it is said,

> He who realizes his manly qualities but keeps womanly qualities as well will have an all-embracing heart like a stream. An all-embracing heart like a stream he who is endowed with eternal virtue will return to the natural state of a newborn baby.

Chapter 38 puts forward the concepts of "superior virtue" and "inferior virtue" by saying,

> A man of superior virtue cares not for superficial virtue, so he is virtuous; a man of inferior virtue cares for superficial virtue, so he is not virtuous.

For the sentence that "a man of superior virtue cares not for superficial virtue, so he is virtuous," "Illustrating Laozi" of *Han Feizi* says, "The mind of a man of superior virtue does not indulge in external things. If the mind does not indulge in external things, the personality will become perfect." In other words, the second word "virtue" in *Laozi* was interpreted as the mind that does not indulge in external things; while the word "virtuous" was interpreted as the "perfect body" (the personality is perfect). This interpretation tended to extend "virtue" to the spiritual aspect, which did not completely conform to Laozi's original intention. Wang Bi said, "A man of superior virtue follows Tao alone. A man of superior virtue does not show his virtue. Therefore, even if he is virtuous, he takes no credit." Compared with that of Han Fei, this interpretation was a step forward, which was much closer to Laozi's original intention. *Laozi* divided "virtue" into two basic levels, namely, "superior virtue" and "inferior virtue." "Superior virtue" was also known as "great virtue," "eternal virtue" or "mystical virtue." In the statement that "A man of superior virtue cares not for superficial virtue, and a man of inferior virtue cares for superficial virtue" in Chapter 38 of *Laozi*, "superficial virtue" was indeed "inferior virtue." In the statements that "so he is virtuous," and "so he is not virtuous" , "virtuous" was supposed to be "superior virtue." Chapter 51 puts "mystical virtue" this way,

"天命之谓性。"❶ 这与老子的"道生之，德畜之"含义相同。不同的是，老子把事物内在的德性称为"德"，而儒家则称为"性"；道家的"德"泛指万物之本质，而儒家的"性"则主要指人的德性。

其次，老子"德"论第二个特点是，老子的所谓"德"也是一个具有不同层次和不同内涵的概念。《老子》第二十一章说："孔德之容，惟道是从。"《老子》第二十八章又说：

知其雄，守其雌，为天下溪。为天下溪，恒德不离；恒德不离，复归于婴儿。

《老子》第三十八章提出"上德"和"下德"的概念：

上德不德，是以有德。下德不失德，是以无德。

《韩非子·解老》说"上德不德，是以有德"，意思是具有"上德"的人精神不游离于外，自身内在的本质就保全了。即把前一个"不德"的"德"，解为不游离在外的"精神"，把"是以有德"的"德"解释为"身全"（自身的本质精神不丢失、得以保全）。这种解释有将"德"往精神方面引申的倾向，似乎不完全符合老子的原意。王弼说："上德之人，唯道是用，不德其德……故虽有德而无德名。"这种解释较韩非前进了一步，更接近老子的原意。因为《老子》一书是把"德"分为两个基本层次的，即"上德"和"下德"。"上德"，又称为"孔德"、"恒德"或者"玄德"。《老子》第三十八章中"上德不德"中的后一个"德"字，实指"下德"；"是以有德"的"德"字应指"上德"；"下德不失德"中所不失的也只能是"下德"；"是以无德"中的"德"字则指"上德"。《老子》第五十一章解释"玄德"说：

❶《中庸》第一章。

❶ Chapter 1 of the *Doctrine of the Mean*.

Giving birth without possessing, working without taking credit and guiding without dominating: This is called "mystical virtue."

To put it in simple words, "mystical virtue" means having virtue without taking credit, which is what Wang Bi said—even if he is virtuous, he takes no credit. Besides "mystical virtue," there are also "the amplest virtue" and "the most powerful virtue" mentioned in Chapter 41.

Corresponding to "superior virtue," "eternal virtue" and "mystical virtue," is "inferior virtue." In Chapter 38 of Wang Bi's *Commentaries on Laozi*, Wang Bi said, "A man of inferior virtue acquires virtue for he is sedulous. He completes things through repeated efforts and propaganda. Then, he will set up the perfect example to govern all things and thus he can gain the name of virtue."

Since "inferior virtue" is such a kind of "virtue," Laozi said, "A man of inferior virtue cares for superficial virtue, so he is not virtuous."

Finally, the third feature of Laozi's so-called "virtue" is what is implied in "The superior virtue seems humble." Chapter 41 says,

The superior virtue seems humble; the purest virtue seems depraved; the amplest virtue seems deficient; the most powerful virtue seems important.

"Mystical virtue" is illustrated by "giving birth without possessing, working without taking credit and guiding without dominating" in Chapter 51, but "humble" is used here to describe "superior virtue." Is it because there is any difference between "superior virtue" and "mystical virtue"? In fact, there is no essential distinction between them. There are only some differences on the surface: Chapter 51 uses descriptive language to clarify the features of "mystical virtue," while Chapter 41 uses vivid figurative language to describe the image of "superior virtue." "Mystical virtue" in Chapter 51 focuses on human behaviors, so it has been interpreted as the virtue of sovereigns or sages throughout history, while "superior virtue" in Chapter 41 focuses on the explanation through natural phenomena, so this "virtue" is not only the virtue of sovereigns and sages, but also the virtue of the whole nature. This virtue completely conforms to the nature of "Tao" and it is also the closest to "Tao," hence, it can be said, "A man of superior virtue follows Tao alone." Therefore, Chapter 28 of *Laozi* compares "eternal virtue" to "a stream." Humble and soft, the stream "flows in places others reject." The statement that "Eternal virtue is an embracing heart like a stream" means that " the superior virtue is humble."

生而不有，为而不恃，长而不宰，是谓玄德。

简单地说，所谓"玄德"就是有功德而不要功德，也就是王弼说的"虽有德而无德名"。除"玄德"之外，《老子》第四十一章还有"广德"、"建德"等名称。

与"上德"、"恒德"、"玄德"相对的，即是"下德"。王弼在《老子注》第三十八章中接着说："下德求而得之，为而成之，则立善以治物，故有德名焉。"

"下德"既然是这样的一种"德"，所以老子说："下德不失德，是以无德。"

再次，老子所谓"德"的第三个特点，是"上德若谷"。《老子》第四十一章说：

上德若谷，大白若辱，广德若不足，建德若偷，质真若渝。

《老子》第五十一章用"生而不有，为而不恃，长而不宰"来说明"玄德"，这里用"若谷"来形容"上德"，"上德"与"玄德"有什么不同吗？二者其实并没有什么本质的区别。区别只在表面：第五十一章是用说明性的语言阐明"玄德"的特征，第四十一章是用生动的譬喻描绘"上德"的形象；第五十一章的"玄德"侧重于人类的行为，故历代多理解为君主或圣人之德，第四十一章的"上德"则侧重以自然现象来说明，因此这种"德"不仅是人类圣君的德行，而且也是整个自然界的品德。这种德行完全符合"道"的品性，离"道"也最近，可以说是"惟道是从"。故《老子》第二十八章又将"恒德"比作"天下溪"。溪，即是溪谷，它谦卑、处下、柔弱，"处众人之所恶"。"恒德"之"为天下溪"，也就是"上德若谷"的意思。

五 无为而治——老子的社会政治思想

Chapter V Governing by Doing Nothing
—Laozi's Socio-political Thought

Sima Qian was a historian of the Western Han Dynasty, whose father, Sima Tan, wrote an article entitled "The Gist of Six Schools." In this article, the masters since the pre-Qin period were classified into different schools in Chinese history for the first time. They were divided into six schools—*Yin* and *Yang*, Confucians, Mohists, Logicians, Legalists, Taoists—and Sima Tan gave the highest evaluation to the Taoist School. He said, "Ideological principles of the Taoist School are simple and easy to follow. Little effort is needed while the effect is great." Later, in "Treatise on Literature" of the *Book of Han*, Ban Gu of the Eastern Han Dynasty summed up the origin and features of the thought of the Taoist School in more concise words, saying that it was "the skill and practice of the noble one, reflecting the principle of ruling the country."

As the historiographer of the Zhou Dynasty, Laozi was supposed to be good at summing up the laws from rises and falls in history, from good and bad fortunes, and from the ancient and the present Tao. However, he was not a pedant who only immersed himself in a heap of old papers; instead, he showed intense concern for the reality. This is implied in Chapter 14 of *Laozi*,

> Govern your country with the ancient Tao, and you will know the origin of all things; this is called "the existence of Tao."

"With the ancient Tao" was written as "with the present Tao" in both Transcript "A" and Transcript "B" of the Mawangdui Silk-book *Laozi*. Some scholars annotating *Laozi* thought that it should be changed into "with the present Tao" to restore the original appearance of the book. However, we do not think that this opinion is acceptable. There are two reasons. For one thing, the latest unearthed Bamboo-slip *Laozi* does not contain this sentence, neither does Chapter 14 of *Laozi* quoted by "Explaining Laozi" of *Han Feizi*, so it is hard to say that "with the ancient Tao" was written as "with the present Tao" in the original version of *Laozi*. For the other thing, ancient people were accustomed to "taking warnings from history." "Announcement of the Duke of Shao" of the *Classic of History* records what Duke Shao of the Western Zhou Dynasty said, "I must take warning from the Xia Dynasty and the Shang Dynasty." The poem, "King Wen" of *Greater Odes* in the *Classic of Poetry*, goes like this

Before Yin (Shang) lost the multitudes,

Its kings were the assessors of God.

Look to Yin as a beacon;

The great appointment is not easily preserved.

In "The Noblemen of the Early Han" of the *Records of the Grand Historian*,

西汉的历史学家司马迁的父亲司马谈，写过一篇在中国历史上第一次对先秦以来的诸子分家分派的文章，题目是《论六家之要指》。在这篇文章中，他把先秦以来的诸子分为阴阳、儒、墨、名、法、道德等六家，并对道家给予了最高的评价。他说，"道家的思想宗旨简约而容易操作，费事少但功效大。"后来，东汉的班固在《汉书·艺文志》中，又用更简明的语言，对道家的思想渊源和特点做出了自己的概括，称道家为"人君南面之术"。

老子是周朝的史官，能从历史上的成败兴亡以及祸福古今之道中总结出规律，这本是他的强项。但是，老子并不只是一位埋头于故纸堆里的学究先生，他是有强烈的现实关怀的。《老子》第十四章说：

执古之道，以御今之有，以知古始，是谓道纪。

"执古之道"一句，马王堆帛书《老子》甲、乙本都写作"执今之道"。有些注释《老子》的学者认为，应该将《老子》中的这一句也改成"执今之道"，恢复《老子》的原貌。我们认为，这种观点是不可取的。理由有两点：第一，最新出土的楚简《老子》中并没有这一段文字，《韩非子·解老》引用了《老子》第十四章的内容，也没有这段话，因此很难说原始的《老子》中"执古之道"应写作"执今之道"；第二，古人有"以古为鉴"的习惯。《尚书·召诰》中，西周初年的召公说："我不能不以夏朝作为借鉴，也不可以不以商朝作为借鉴。"《诗经》中的《大雅·文王》一诗说："殷朝的军队没有消灭的时候，它能够配得上给上帝的祭祀，但现在它也被灭亡了。所以应该以殷人为鉴，要知道天命不容易保持，我们的江山也不一定永远不会失去。"司马迁在《史记·高祖功臣侯者年表序》

Sima Qian said, "In today's society, to bear in mind the ancient experience and lessons is to take warning from history." Only Legalists said, "There is no definite way in a well-governed society, so the present society should not follow the example of the ancient" ;❶ "Talking about the remote antiquity while brushing aside the present sovereign is just like serving others' sovereign while ignoring one's own." ❷ Therefore, "governing your country with the ancient Tao" should be Laozi's original intention, while the change from "ancient" into "present" was probably made by the people who had Legalist tendency in the Warring States Period.

Thus, Laozi talked about "Tao" and "virtue," and eagerly summed up "the Tao of the ancient times," with a view of solving problems in reality and extracting a set of recipes for governing the people and making them at peace.

Laozi lived in the late Spring and Autumn and the early Warring States periods, when there were great changes and turmoil. His socio-political thought of governing the people and making them at peace was aimed at the social reality at the time.

Chapter 75 of *Laozi* says,

> The people are difficult to govern, and the rulers interfere too much; therefore, the people are difficult to govern.

Here, Laozi examined the politics in the realistic society from two aspects— the rulers and the people. In the realistic society, the people seemed to be a gang of "unruly people," who were difficult to govern. But, according to Laozi, the rulers, rather than the people, should be blamed. Why should the rulers be blamed? According to Wang Bi's *Commentaries on Laozi*, it is because the people followed the example of their rulers. In today's words, the people learn from and follow the cadres. Therefore, throughout history, both Confucianism and Taoism have emphasized that the officials should set a good example for the people, rather than issue orders to them. Confucius said, "When a prince's personal conduct is correct, his government is effective without the issuing of

中说："生活在当今社会，心里牢记古代的经验教训，是为了以古代为借鉴。"只有法家人物才说："治理得好的社会没有一定的方法，便于当今社会就不要效法古代。"❶ "舍弃当代的君主而谈论上古，就好象舍弃自己的国君去事奉别人的国君。"❷ 所以，"执古之道"以治理今天的国家，应该就是老子的原句，而改为"执今之道"，很可能是战国时期有法家思想倾向的人改动的。

所以，老子谈"道"论"德"，汲汲于总结"古之道术"的目的，是为了解决现实社会的种种问题，是为了提炼出一套治国安民的良方。

老子所处的时代，是中国的春秋末期到战国初期，那是一个大变革、大动荡的时代。老子治国安民的社会政治思想，就是针对当时的社会现实而发的。

《老子》第七十五章说：

> 民之难治也，以其上之有为，是以难治。

这里，老子是从"上"（即统治者）与"民"（即老百姓、人民）两个方面来考察现实社会的政治的。在现实社会中，人民似乎都成了一群"刁民"，很难对付和治理了。但老子认为，这不是老百姓的过错，过错在"上"，即在统治者。为什么说过错在统治者呢？王弼的《老子注》说："这是因为民从上。"用今天的话说，就是老百姓都学习和仿效官员。所以，中国自古以来就强调官员们要以身作则，给老百姓做好的表率，而不是忙着对人民发号施令。不管儒家、道家都是这样。孔子说："当官的自身做好了，不发布命令老百姓就会跟着走正道；如果官吏

❶《史记·商君列传》。
❷《荀子·非相》。

❶ "The Biography of Kings in the Shang Dgnasty," in the *Records of the Grand Historian.*
❷ "Feixiang," *Xunzi.*

orders. If his personal conduct is not correct, he may issue orders, but they will not be followed." ❶ Chapter 2 of *Laozi* also says, the sage "teaches without verbal instruction."

However, the real situation was not like that. The fact was that "the rulers interfered too much and the people were difficult to govern." What are "interfere too much" and "difficult to govern" ? Heshanggong's *Commentaries on Laozi* in the Western Han Dynasty says, "The reason why the people are difficult to govern is that the present rulers desire excessively and like making interference at will. The people are so misled that they also have more desires and resort to deception. Therefore, they are difficult to govern." It is obvious that "interfere too much" does not mean that the rulers did what they should do, instead, it means that they desired too much, asked for trouble and acted blindly. "Difficult to govern" means that the people no longer behaved themselves and became difficult to govern. According to Laozi, the rulers and their "interfering too much" should be blamed, while the people were just victims. Chapter 53 of *Laozi* says,

> Still some people are clad in grand clothes, carry sharp weapons, indulge in grand food, and overflow with excessive wealth: They can properly be called " master thieves."

Laozi said angrily, "They are showing off the goods which were robbed from the people." Sighing that "the people are difficult to govern," Laozi also pointed out in sharp terms in Chapter 75,

> The people are starving: The rulers are guilty of over-taxation; therefore, the people are starving. The people are taking death lightly: The rulers are luxuriously self-indulgent; therefore, the people are taking death lightly.

Therefore, Chapter 74 asks rhetorically, "If people do not fear death, why bother threatening them with it?" In other words, the rulers should look for the causes from themselves. Instead of threatening the people blindly with death, they should be aware that their own "excessive desires," "interfering too much" and "being master thieves" led to the revolt of the people.

According to Laozi, the rulers' "excessive desires" and "interfering too much" not only made it hard for the people to survive, forcing them to risk danger in desperation, but also led to frequent wars between the vassal states, worsening the suffering of the people. Chapter 46 says, "When Tao is absent from the world, colts are bred on the battlefields." Chapter 30 also says,

自身不走正道，即使三令五申老百姓也不会听他们的。" ❶
《老子》第二章也说，圣人"行不言之教。"

但是，现实的情形却不是这样。现实是"上有为而民难治"。
什么叫"有为"和"难治"呢？西汉河上公的《老子注》说：
"人民之所以难治的原因，就在于现在的统治者欲望太多，喜
欢乱作为。老百姓受了他们的误导，也欲望多、弄虚作假而难
以治理。"可见，"有为"不是他管了该管的事，而是说他欲望
太多，没事找事，瞎折腾。"难治"，就是人人都不再安分守己，
不好管理了。老子认为，这里主要责任在统治者，在他们是
"有为"，而老百姓则是受害者。《老子》第五十三章说：

服文采，带利剑，厌饮食，财货有余，是为盗夸。

老子愤怒地说："这些都是从老百姓那里抢劫来的，是在
夸耀他们的盗窃品。"《老子》第七十五章在感叹"民之难治"
的同时，还尖锐地指出：

人之饥，以其上食税之多，是以饥。……民之轻死，
以其上求生之厚，是以轻死。

所以《老子》第七十四章反问道："民不畏死，奈何以死
惧之？"即是说统治者应该从自己身上找找现在"民之难治"
的原因，要看到他们自己"多欲"、"有为"、"盗夸"，才是老
百姓反抗的根源；而不要一味地用杀戮恐吓老百姓。老百姓求
生不得，是不怕死的，因而用杀戮恐吓老百姓是无用的。

老子还认为，统治者的"多欲"、"有为"，不仅使人民生
存艰难，逼得人民铤而走险，而且还导致了诸侯国之间频繁的
战争，加深了人民的苦难。《老子》第四十六章说："天下无道，
战争连年，使母马在郊野生产下马驹。"第三十章又说："军队

❶《论语·子路》。

❶ "Zilu," *Lunyu.*

"Where troops are stationed, thorns and brambles grow. In the sequence of large-scale wars there are sure to be bad years."

Laozi lived in the turbulent times when the whole country was in chaos, with people living in dire poverty. The situation, in the eyes of Confucians, is what was called "The sovereign was not sovereign, the minister was not minister, the father was not father, and the son was not son" and nobody behaved themselves. The "norms of propriety" played a dominant role in the late Spring and Autumn Period. The so-called "collapse of propriety and music" does not mean that the "norms of propriety and music" should be totally discarded. On the contrary, it only means that it was the time of great changes when most of the norms had been broken and needed restoring. Therefore, both Confucianism and Taoism turned to the "norms of propriety" when they were discussing the realistic issues of the time. For example, when Confucius consulted Laozi about the rites, Confucius proposed that the solution to the social conflicts should be to restore the norms of propriety of Zhou. Confucius said, "Zhou had the advantage of viewing the two past dynasties. How complete and elegant are its regulations! I follow Zhou." ❶ Yet, he also held that equal importance should be attached to the norms of propriety and music as well as inherent "benevolence." There was no shortage of the external forms of propriety and music in the society, but they were just the hypocritical form because of the lack of inherent respect and the basis of inherent benevolence. Thus, Confucius also said, "If a man is without the virtues proper to humanity, what has he to do with the rites of propriety? If a man is without the virtues proper to humanity, what has he to do with music?" ❷ "'It is according to the rules of propriety,' they say. 'It is according to the rules of propriety,' they say. Are gems and silk all that is meant by propriety? 'It is music,' they say. Are bells and drums all that is meant by music?" ❸ By this, Confucius meant that propriety and music existed for nothing without benevolence from people.

Confronted with the social chaos, Laozi also firstly looked for the reasons from "propriety." He said in Chapter 38,

Once righteousness is lost, propriety arises. Propriety signifies the loss of loyalty and faith; it is the beginning of disorder.

These words are generally believed to express Laozi's thought of opposing propriety. In regard to this, however, we suggest that we should make a detailed analysis of this point, rather than be limited to the general view.

In the light of his life, Laozi was pretty much acquainted with "propriety," because he once was the historiographer of the Zhou Dynasty and explained it

经过而且发生过战争的地方，往往都变得残破不堪、荆棘丛生；一次大的战争之后，一定会伴随着饥荒年份的到来。"

老子所处的时代，是一个国家混乱、民不聊生的大动荡时代。这种情形，用儒家的眼光来看，就是所谓"君不君、臣不臣、父不父、子不子"，从上到下都乱套了。因为，在春秋之前，中国社会发挥统治作用的机制是"礼"制。所谓"礼崩乐坏"，是指原有的礼乐制度有很多遭到了破坏，需要修复。所以，不论是儒家还是道家，在讨论当时的现实问题时，就都把目光投向了"礼"。孔子向老子问礼，孔子提出的解决社会矛盾的方法就是恢复周礼。他说："周监于二代（夏、殷），郁郁乎文哉；吾从周。"❶但孔子又认为，恢复礼乐制度应该与内在的"仁德"并重才行。现实社会不是没有礼乐的外在形式，但由于缺少内在的礼敬，没有内在的仁德为内涵，所以这些礼乐制度都成了虚伪的形式、外在的躯壳。故孔子又说："人而不仁，如礼何？人而不仁，如乐何？"❷"礼云礼云，玉帛云乎哉？乐云乐云，钟鼓云乎哉？"❸意思是说，人如果没有仁爱之心，礼乐就没有什么意义了。

老子面对当时社会的混乱，也首先从"礼"那里寻找原因。他说（第三十八章）：

夫礼者，忠信之薄，而乱之首也。

老子的这几句，通常被认为表达了老子反对礼的思想。我们认为，对这一点应该作具体的分析，不可笼统地看。

从老子的生平来看，他是周朝的史官，曾给孔子讲解过礼

❶《论语·八佾》。
❷《论语·八佾》。
❸《论语·阳货》。

❶ "Bayi," *Lunyu.*
❷ "Bayi," *Lunyu.*
❸ "Yang Huo," *Lunyu.*

to Confucius. Naturally, he also knew that "propriety" was the essential code of conduct and systematic norm that maintained the normal social order. But the fact is that "propriety" did not bring order, norms or harmony to the society; instead, it led to a variety of chaos and disputes. Therefore, out of indignation, Laozi said, "Once righteousness is lost, propriety arises. Propriety signifies the loss of loyalty and faith; it is the beginning of disorder."

On the other hand, there was a prerequisite when Laozi said this. Laozi once divided "propriety" into two kinds: the "propriety" with both connotation and form and the formalistic "propriety" without real connotation. He was only opposed to the latter. As he once instructed Confucius about the "propriety," there was no reason that he could not understand Confucius' question that "Are bells and drums all that is meant by music?" According to him, "propriety" was the culprit of the realistic society. This is, in fact, his criticism and denial of the realistic society, which was in disorder with endless calamities, and this is also his logical starting point for the examination of the social politics and historical trends.

This is the social reality Laozi was confronted with, which developed farther and farther away from "Tao" and "virtue." Laozi was worried about and angry with this. Chapter 20 says,

> Other people are happy and gay, as if attending a grand sacrificial feast, or climbing a terrace on a fine spring day. I stand alone, with a blank look on my face, like a newborn baby who has not yet learned to smile. Limply I wander like a homeless waif.

How to change the chaotic and miserable social reality, which was farther away from "Tao" and "virtue" ? At the bottom of his heart, Laozi pinned his hope on the "sages" or the rulers who possessed "Tao" and "virtue" like them.

Throughout *Laozi*, the word "sage" appears 32 times in all, while in the *Analects*, both "virtuous" and "sage" appear only 4 times respectively. It is obvious that the "sage" is the ideal personality in Laozi's thought.

What are "sages" like? They are the ones with the loftiest "Tao" and "virtue." According to Laozi, they are the ones who "embrace Tao and virtue." Of course, at the same time, they must be in the position of "the Son of Heaven" or the ruler so that they can govern the world.

"Following Tao alone" and governing by doing nothing are essential for

的学问，这说明他对"礼"是十分熟悉的。他自然也懂得"礼"是维护正常社会秩序的基本的行为准则和制度规范。但现实的情况是，"礼"不仅没有给社会带来秩序、规范与和谐，还导致了各种混乱与纷争。所以，老子才一时激愤，说出了"夫礼者，忠信之薄，而乱之首也"的话来。

另一方面，老子讲这番话是有前提的。老子曾将"礼"分为两类：内涵与形式相统一的"礼"和失掉了实质内涵而流于形式的"礼"。他只反对徒具形式的"礼"，因为老子作为曾为孔子指教过"礼"的人，他不可能连孔子所谓"礼乐不等于外在的玉帛和钟鼓等礼器"的道理都不懂得。他之所以说"礼"是现实社会的罪魁祸首，这实际是他对秩序混乱、灾难连绵的现实社会的一种批判和否定，是他考察社会政治、历史潮流的逻辑起点。

老子所面对的现实社会，是一个离"道"、"德"越来越远的社会。老子对此充满了忧虑和愤慨。《老子》第二十章说：

众人熙熙，如享太牢，如登春台。我独泊兮其未兆，如婴儿之未孩，儽儽兮若无所归。

如何才能改变这种远离"道"、"德"的混乱而苦难的社会现实呢？老子把希望寄托于"圣人"或如圣人那样有"道"、"德"的统治者。

在《老子》一书中，"圣人"一词共出现了三十二次，而在儒家的《论语》中"圣"字仅出现四次，"圣人"也只出现过四次。可见，"圣人"是老子思想中的理想人格。

"圣人"是什么样的人呢？他们是"道"、"德"最高的人。用老子的话说，他们是"同于道"、"同于德"的人。当然，他们同时也必须处于"天子"或君主的位置，可以治理天下。

"圣人"治理天下，根本的一条就是要"唯道是从"，无为

the "sage" to govern the world. Chapter 2 says,

> Therefore, the sage acts without visible action; he teaches without verbal instruction. He observes growth without activating it; he works without claiming credit; he succeeds without dwelling upon it.

The "sage" is the embodiment of "the mighty Tao" and "the mystical virtue," governing the world on behalf of "Tao" and "virtue." Laozi said, "When nothing is done at all, nothing is left undone" (Chapter 37); "Giving birth without possessing, working without taking credit and guiding without dominating: This is called 'mystical virtue' " (Chapter 51).

"Governing by doing nothing" is the general principle for the "sage" to deal with all things and govern the country. The general principle also contains a number of specific contents and rules for the operation. For example, the sage's requirement for himself is not identical with that for the viscounts and dukes, while his requirement for the people is even more distinct.

In terms of the standard the "sage" sets for himself, the "sage" should regard "the mighty Tao" and "the mystical Tao" as the model, and "govern by doing nothing," as void and humble as the mountains, streams and seas. Chapter 28 says, "He who realizes his manly qualities but keeps womanly qualities as well will have an all-embracing heart like a stream. He who realizes his innocence but bears humiliation will have an all-embracing heart like a valley." This actually means that the "sage" should stay humble and weak and bear humiliation as the brooks and streams, because "Tao in the world is like rivers and seas, into which all brooks and streams flow." People will be closer to "Tao" if they "benefit everything and remain still and flow in places others reject" like water. "Superior virtue" is also like the brooks and streams, so the "sage" will first pattern after the nature if he wants to govern the world and achieve great success. Chapter 34 says,

> Therefore, the sage becomes great because he never considers himself great; this is how his greatness is achieved.

Modest and humble, the "sage" neither does anything nor competes with others, which is known as "the sage's outer appearance belying his inner worth" (Chapter 70). In Chapter 66, Laozi said, "The sea is the king of countless streams because it lies below them; lowliness makes it the lord of streams. If the sage is to guide the people, he must speak in modest terms; if the sage is to lead the people, he must follow behind. Therefore, the sage leads without doing harm and guides without being oppressive. The people support him

而治。《老子》第二章说：

> 是以圣人处无为之事，行不言之教。万物作焉而弗辞，
> 生而不有，为而弗恃，功成而弗居。

"圣人"就是"大道"和"玄德"的化身，代表着"道"、"德"治理天下。而老子说："道常无为而无不为"（第三十七章）；"生而不有，为而不恃，长而不宰，是为玄德"（第五十一章）。

"无为而治"是"圣人"应对万物、治理国家的总原则。在这种总的原则之下，还包含了许多具体的操作细则和内容。比如对"圣人"自己的要求和对王侯、王公的要求就不一样，对老百姓的要求更不相同。

就"圣人"对自己的标准而言，"圣人"要处处以"大道"和"玄德"为楷模，如山川、溪谷、江海那样虚怀、谦卑、处下、"无为而无不为"。《老子》第二十八章说："知其雄，守其雌，为天下溪"；"知其荣，守其辱，为天下谷。"这实际是说"圣人"应如溪谷那样保持谦卑柔弱、含垢忍辱。因为"道之在天下，犹川谷之与江海也"。如果人能如水那样，"善利万物而不争，处众人之所恶"，就能接近于"道"。而"上德"也如溪谷一样，所以"圣人"治天下，做出天下伟业，首先就要效法"自然"。《老子》第三十四章说：

> 圣人之能成其大也，以其终不自为大，故能成其大。

"圣人"谦卑、处下、不争、无为，这叫作"圣人被褐而怀玉"（第七十章）。老子说："江海之所以能成为各种溪谷的王，就因为它善于处下，所以它能成为百谷之王。因此圣人要想位居民众之上，就必须言语谦卑；虽然身居民众之前，但一定要退居民众之后而谦让不争。这样就可以身居上位而民众并不感到负担加重，身居民众之前而民众并不感到妨害。天下的

ungrudgingly. He does not compete with others, so no one competes with him."
The sage's principle of life is no other than what is implied in Laozi's words,
"He who grasps the immense image of Tao travels worldwide" (Chapter 35).

To govern the world is how to face the previous political system and
norms of morality. Laozi thought that the original norms of etiquette
(humaneness, righteousness, propriety and wisdom) and norms of morality
were produced by their gradual alienation from "Tao" and "the mystical
virtue," and thus, they were problematic. So, Chapter 18 says,

> When the mighty Tao is discarded, humaneness and righteousness
> arise; when people begin to live by their wits, deception and hypocrisy
> arise; when family ties begin to unravel, dutifulness and benevolence arise;
> when the country is in chaos and confusion, loyalty and patriotism arise.

There has been much controversy about this chapter throughout history.
According to most people, it showed that Laozi was opposed to humaneness and
righteousness. However, the Silk-book *Laozi* and the Bamboo-slip *Laozi* had the
word "how" before the sentences containing "arise," so the viewpoint that Laozi
was not against humaneness, righteousness, loyalty and dutifulness seemingly got
the upper hand. As a matter of fact, Laozi only explained the origin and
development of "Tao" and its relationship with humaneness, righteousness,
wisdom, dutifulness, benevolence, loyalty and patriotism. His intention was
identical to what he said in "Once Tao is lost, virtue arises; once virtue is lost,
humaneness arises." Even if "how" was added, the origin and development of
"the mighty Tao," humaneness and righteousness were not changed. If Laozi really
opposed to the existing social value norms, it was just because they were separated
from "the mighty Tao" and got farther away from it. Therefore, Chapter 19 says,

> Eliminate formalized wisdom and learning, and the people will benefit
> a hundredfold; eliminate hypocritical humaneness and righteousness, and
> the people will restore dutifulness and benevolence; eliminate trickery and
> profiteering, and the people will have no thieves to fear.

Wang Bi's *Commentaries on Laozi* says, "Formalized wisdom and
learning are the best part of one's talent; humaneness and righteousness are the
most excellent part of one's nature; trickery and profiteering are the most
concerned part of one's conduct." ❶ It is said that the Bamboo-slip *Laozi*
records, "Eliminate learning and polemic and the people will benefit a
hundredfold; eliminate trickery and profiteering, and the people will have no
thieves to fear; eliminate hypocrisy and worries and the people will restore

人都乐意推举他成为君王而不厌烦他。这不就是因为他谦卑处下、无欲不争，天下才没有谁能与他相争吗？"（第六十六章）"圣人"这一处世规则，老子把它叫作"执大象，天下往。"（第三十五章）

"圣人"治理天下，还有一个如何面对以往既有的政治制度、道德规范的问题。老子认为，原有的仁、义、礼、智这些礼制和道德规范，是逐渐远离"大道"与"玄德"的产物，所以是有问题的。《老子》第十八章说：

> 大道废，有仁义；智慧出，有大伪；六亲不和，有孝慈；国家昏乱，有忠臣。

对于老子的这段话，历来争论也很大，而认为老子反对仁义的人居多。但是帛书《老子》和楚简《老子》中的"有"字前都有一个"安"（焉）字，于是认为老子不反对仁、义、忠、孝的观点，似乎又占了上风。实际上，老子这里只是对仁义、智慧、孝慈、忠臣与"大道"的源流关系作出了说明，与"失道而后德，失德而后仁"的思路是相同的。老子反对仁、义、礼、知、忠、信等既有的社会价值规范，只是因为它们与"大道"分离，且与"大道"渐行渐远了。故《老子》第十九章说：

> 绝圣弃智，民利百倍；绝仁弃义，民复孝慈；绝巧弃利，盗贼无有。

王弼《老子注》说："圣、智，才之善者；仁、义，行之善者；巧、利，用之善者。"❶有人指出在楚简《老子》甲组中这段话写作："绝智弃辩，民利百倍；绝巧弃利，盗贼无

---

❶ 王弼：《老子注》第十九章。

❶ Chapter 19 of *Commentaries on Laozi* by Wang Bi.

dutifulness and benevolence." According to this, some people thought that Laozi was not against "humaneness, righteousness, formalized wisdom and learning." As a matter of fact, it is not necessary to say so. In any case, Laozi only "respected Tao and honored virtue," and except that, is there anything that he was completely satisfied with?

The essential question for the "sage" to govern the world is, of course, how to treat the people.

According to Laozi, the "sage" should first regard the people as the basis for the existence of a nation, that is, he should be people-oriented. In Chapter 49, Laozi said, "The sage never nurtures prejudice or bias; his heart resonates with his people's hearts." In Chapter 39, he said, "The superior must depend upon the inferior for support; the high must depend upon the low as its base." Accordingly, the humble people should be seen as the basis of a national power. It is noteworthy that being people-oriented does not mean keeping the people on the go all day long, or letting them continually gain new knowledge and improve their literacy. In contrast, it means making the people also "do nothing" — "abstain from intellectualism and desire." So, Chapter 3 says,

> Not honoring wise men keeps people from dissension; not valuing rare goods keeps people from thievery; not stimulating desires keeps people from confusion. Therefore, the sage governs his people by emptying their minds and filling their stomachs, weakening their wills and strengthening their bones. If the people abstain from intellectualism and desire and are convinced not to aspire, order will always prevail.

It is obvious that the sage's "doing nothing" is consistent with that of the people. This is what Laozi said in Chapter 57, "I take no action and people become honest; I enjoy quietness and people become peaceful; I meddle not in busy affairs and people become rich; I desire no desires and people become simple and good." In contrast, if the sages "take action," "meddle in busy affairs" and "have desires," showing off their "sharp weapons," "knowledge" and "laws and orders," the people's desires will be aroused and they will compete for profits, pursue trickery and even become thieves and robbers without any fear of death. To induce the people with petty favors or things that can arouse their desires seems to be of benevolence to them, but in fact, it scourges them. Laozi said, "Heaven and earth are inhumane, indifferent to everything like worthless straw-dog sacrifices; the sage is inhumane, indifferent to everyone like worthless straw-dog sacrifices" (Chapter 5). In the old times, straw-dog sacrifices would be thrown away after the ceremony. "The

有；绝伪弃虑，民复孝慈。"其中无"仁"、"义"、"圣"等字，就认为老子是不反对"仁、义、圣、智"的。这样说也是没有必要的。因为老子只是"尊道而贵德"，除此之外，有什么是他完全满意的呢？

当然，"圣人"治理天下，最基本的还是如何对待人民或百姓的问题。

老子认为，"圣人"对待人民，首先是应该把老百姓看作一个国家存在的基础，即以民为本。老子说"圣人常无心，以百姓心为心。"（第四十九章）"贵以贱为本，高以下为基。"（第三十九章）因此，应该把地位卑贱的民众作为国家政权存在的基础，并不是要像儒家那样对人民实行仁政，而是要使老百姓也"无为"，即"无知无欲"。《老子》第三章说：

> 不尚贤，使民不争；不贵难得之货，使民不为盗；不见可欲，使民心不乱。是以圣人之治，虚其心，实其腹，弱其志，强其骨。常使民无知无欲，使夫智者不敢为也。为无为，则无不治。

看来，"圣人"的"无为"和老百姓的"无为"也是统一的，用老子自己的话来说，这叫作"我无为而民自化，我好静而民自正，我无事而民自富，我无欲而民自朴。"（第五十七章）相反，统治者"有为"、"有事"、"有欲"，弄来一些"利器"、"伎巧"、"法令"在老百姓面前炫耀，勾起了人民的种种欲望，就会使老百姓争利谋诈，乃至不怕死而偷盗。用一点小恩小惠引诱人民，表面上好像对人民充满仁爱，实际则是在祸害百姓。老子说："天地不仁，以万物为刍狗；圣人不仁，以百姓为刍狗。"（第五章）刍狗是古代祭祀时用草扎成的道具，用完就扔掉。《庄子·天运》说，泉水干涸的时候，鱼儿们在陆地上为

Revolution of Heaven" of *Zhuangzi* records, "When the springs (supplying the pools) are dried up, the fishes huddle together on the dry land. Than that they should moisten one another there by their gasping, and keep one another wet by their milt, it would be better for them to forget one another in the rivers and lakes." Therefore, Wang Anshi of the Song Dynasty said, "He who loves people without resorting to love will keep his status longer." ❶ Thus, Laozi also said, "When government is lenient, people become simple and good; when government is harsh, people become cunning and evil" (Chapter 58); "A follower of Tao aims not to enlighten the people but to keep them in the dark" (Chapter 65). This shows that only by "doing nothing," "having no desires" and "not meddling in busy affairs" can the "sage" make the people become simple and good.

The sage is, of course, integrated with "the mighty Tao" and "the mystical virtue." He "governs a large country as if cooking a small fish" (Chapter 60) and he is not going to or does not have to attend to everything himself. Laozi thought that the lords, princes, dukes, clans and even nobles really exerted the national authority at the time. Besides, according to him, "The world is an integrated whole at the beginning, and undergoes the phase in which uncarved wood breaks down to be used for vessel" and then "returns to the simple state of uncarved wood again." It is the inevitable result of "reversion being the way of Tao." Therefore, the military officer is also indispensable. Chapter 28 says,

> When uncarved wood breaks down to be used for vessel, the sage
> uses them, like an officer.

Wang Bi's *Commentaries on Laozi* says, "Being uncarved is the real state of all things. When the real state is discrete, all walks of life and different things are created, just like substance. By virtue of the separation of the things, the sage appoints officers for all walks of life. He employs people with good virtue as teachers and people with bad conduct as resources, transforms the outmoded habits and customs and makes the world return to its simplicity." ❷

It is self-evident that the lords, princes, dukes, clans and nobles were teachers with good virtue. Laozi mentioned many times, "Lords and princes have thus been solemnized;" "An unqualified lord or prince is likely to fall;" "Lords and princes refer to themselves as 'Lonely,' 'Forlorn' and 'Worthless' ; this means that they depend upon their subjects for support" (Chapter 39). "All things detest what is lonely, forlorn, or worthless; nevertheless, this is how lords and princes refer to themselves" (Chapter 42). "Tao is eternal and nameless. If lords and princes adhere to it, everything will follow its natural way" (Chapter 37). "A follower of Tao, in his service to a ruler, will oppose the

了活命互相挤在一起吐口沫哈湿气，好像很相爱，倒不如在江湖里各游各的，互不关心。所以宋代的王安石说："爱民者，以不爱爱之，乃长。"❶ 老子又说："其政闷闷，其民淳淳；其政察察，其民缺缺。"（第五十八章）"古之善为道者，非以明民，将以愚之。"（第六十五章）说的都是统治者要通过自己的"无为"、"无欲"、"无事"，使老百姓纯朴守真。

当然，圣人是与"大道"、"玄德"同体的，他们"治大国若烹小鲜"（第六十章），是不会也不必事事躬亲的。老子觉得当时真正行使国家权力的，是王侯、公卿乃至士一类的在上位者。而且，老子认为，天下由最初的混然为一，经过"朴散为器"，再"复归于朴"，是"反者道之动"的必然结果。所以官长也是必不可少的。《老子》第二十八章说：

朴散为器，圣人用之，则为官长。

王弼的注释说："朴，就是事物本真的状态。本真的状态分开离散了，那么各行各业、不同的事类就产生了，就好像器物一样。圣人借助事物的分离，为各行各业来建立官长。用品德好的人做教师，用品行不良的人为资源，移风易俗，使天下重新回归于纯真。"❷

显然，王侯、公卿、士就是"为师"的品德好的人。老子多次说道："侯王得一以为天下正"；"侯王无以高，将恐蹶"；"侯王自谓孤、寡、不谷，此非以贱为本邪！"（第三十九章）"人之所恶，唯孤、寡、不谷，而王公以为称"（第四十二章）；"道常无为而无不为，侯王若能守之，万物将自化"（第三十七章）；"以道佐人主者，不以兵强天下"（第三十

❶ 彭耜:《老子道德经集注》引。
❷ 王弼:《老子注》第二十八章。

❶ Peng Si, Quotation from *Selected Commentaries on Laozi*.
❷ Chapter 28 of *Commentaries on Laozi* by Wang Bi.

use of armed forces to conquer the world" (Chapter 30) and "The ancient sages who were followers of Tao were miraculously perceptive and unfathomly profound" (Chapter 15). It is such a kind of officer that Laozi hoped to lead people return to simplicity.

According to his own principles of "respecting Tao and honoring virtue," Laozi put forward the socio-political thought and claims. But this does not mean that if his political thought and claims were put into practice, the realistic society of the time would match his ideal. Chapter 28 uses three "return" s successively to show the aim of the "sage," that is, "return to the natural state of a newborn baby," "return to the perfect state of infinity" and "return to the simple state of uncarved wood." It can be summarized in one sentence, that is to say, return to the original state of "Tao" and "virtue." In Chapter 80, Laozi gave a specific account of his social thought:

> The ideal country is small with few people. The people have efficient tools but no one uses them; they take life and death seriously and no one travels afar. Though they have boats and carts, no one rides them; though they have armor and weapons, no one displays them; they return to the use of knotted cords for memoranda. They relish fine food; they admire beautiful clothes; they delight in traditional customs; they relax in comfortable homes. Neighboring countries are within sight of one another; sounds of crowing cocks and barking dogs fill the air; yet the people never come and go—they simply grow old and die.

The social scene described by Laozi is really fantastic, which has attracted the reverie of numerous people throughout history. For example, Zhuangzi wrote, "In the age of perfect virtue, people filled their mouths with food and were glad; they slapped their stomachs to express their satisfaction." Bao Jingyan of the Western Jin Dynasty expressed his yearning for the free life in *No Monarch*, in which there were no monarch or officials and people lived in peace and worked happily. Tao Yuanming in the Eastern Jin Dynasty described in "The Fountain of the Peach Blossom Spring" that roads and paths crisscrossing the fields in all directions, the crowing of cocks and the barking of dogs were within everyone's earshot. All these descriptions should be said to have made constant sequels to *Laozi*. However, these scenes are, of course, nothing but the mirage. Though beautiful, they are always illusory and elusive.

章）；"古之善为士者，微妙玄通，深不可识"（第十五章）等等。老子就是希望这样的官长引导人民复归于朴。

老子按照他的"尊道贵德"的原则，提出了一套社会政治思想和主张。《老子》第二十八章连用了三个"复归"来说明"圣人"的目的，即"复归于婴儿"、"复归于无极"、"复归于朴"。一句话，回到"道"、"德"的原初状态。《老子》第八十章具体描述了他的这一社会理想：

> 小国寡民，使有什佰之器而不用，使民重死不远徙。虽有舟舆，无所乘之；虽有甲兵，无所陈之。使民复结绳而用之。甘其食，美其服，安其居，乐其俗。邻国相望，鸡犬之声相闻，民至老死不相往来。

老子描述的这一社会图景的确非常美妙，引起来古往今来许多人的无限遐想。庄子笔下至德之世的人们熙熙而乐、鼓腹而游的生活，西晋鲍敬言《无君论》中对无君无吏、人们安土乐业的自由生活的憧憬，东晋陶渊明《桃花源记》中阡陌相连、鸡犬之声相闻的风景——应该说，这些都是在不断地为《老子》写作续篇。当然，这些图景也正如海市蜃楼一般，虽然很美，却永远虚无缥缈，可望而不可及。

老子的思想造成了后世文人的"出世"观念
The idea of alienation of Chinese scholars
influenced by Laozi's thought

六　知足知止——老子的人生哲学思想

Chapter Ⅵ　He Who Is Contented Knows What to Avoid
—Laozi's Philosophy of Life

Generally speaking, compared with the Western philosophical thought that focuses on logic and reasoning, the traditional Chinese philosophical thought places more emphasis on social and life issues. In this sense, it can be said that the traditional Chinese philosophy is mainly a philosophy of life.

Such is the case with Laozi's philosophical thought. Then, how did Laozi put forward the solutions to the relationship between an individual and others, the individual and his own body and mind? Or what ideal and attitude to life did Laozi think the individual should adopt to realize the harmony between himself and the society and that between his body and mind?

Laozi's elaboration on those above questions is his philosophy of life.

1. Which Is More Precious, Your Name or Life?

Laozi's philosophical thought starts with the elaboration on the root, development and formation of all things. He regarded "the mighty Tao" as the root of all things in the universe. According to him, the world was formed in this way, "From Tao comes oneness; from oneness comes the duality of *yin* and *yang*; from duality comes the equilibrium of *yin* and *yang*; from equilibrium come all things under heaven."

The above is a general description. If in terms of each individual, the process of his coming into existence should be as follows, "Tao gives birth to and virtue nurtures all things; existence takes shape and things are completed" (Chapter 51). Some people might say that each specific "individual" is produced by his own mother. This is, of course, the case. But, as an "individual" of human beings, "he" is also a member of the trio of "heaven," "earth" and "man." Therefore, in the final analysis, "he" is produced by "Tao" and his humanity is granted by "virtue." However, only by the condensation of *yin* and *yang* (the so-called "vital breath" in general), can the "individual" become a human being. After his birth, he eats the grains and then grows into a human body.

Laozi's philosophical thought as a whole, including socio-political doctrine and philosophy of life, is centered on "respecting Tao and honoring virtue." The sage is like this, let alone the common people. In brief, the basic

一般地讲，与重视逻辑和理性的西方哲学思想相比，中国传统的哲学思想更侧重于对社会和人生问题的探讨。从这个意义上来说，中国传统的哲学，可以说主要是一种人生哲学。

老子的哲学思想也是这样的。那么，老子提出的处理个人与他人、以及个人与自己的身心之间关系的方案是怎样的呢？或者说，老子认为一个人应该以一种怎样的人生理想和生活态度，来实现其个人与社会、以及个人自身的身心的和谐呢？

老子在这方面的论述，体现了他的人生哲学思想。

（一）名与身孰亲？

老子的哲学思想是从论天地万物的根源、发生和形成开始的。他把"大道"看作宇宙万物的总根源，世界是以"道生一，一生二，二生三，三生万物"的模式形成的。"道"生出"有"、"无"统一的"一"来，这叫"道生一"；"一"又产生出阴阳"二"气，这叫"一生二"；"阴阳"二气的结合便产生出"天、地、人"来，这叫"二生三"；天、地加上人的劳动，进一步产生自然和人类社会的万事万物。

以上是从总体上说的。如果从每一个个体来看，他的形成过程就应是："道生之，德畜之，物形之，器（势）成之。"（第五十一章）也许有人会说，每个具体的"人"，都是由他的母亲所生。这当然是对的。但从作为人类的"人"来看，"他"又是"天、地、人"这个"三"中之一。所以在根本上"他"是由"道"所生，并被"德"赋予了"他"的人性。但"人"还必须由具体的阴阳之气（也就是通常所谓"血气"）凝结成人出生后再吃五谷杂粮，生长成人的身体。

老子的整个哲学思想，包括社会政治学说和人生哲学，都围绕一个中心展开，那就是："尊道而贵德"。圣人尚且如此，

principle of his philosophy of life is to require people to depend on "the mighty Tao" and "the mystical virtue" to cultivate their bodies and minds, to get along with others, "to be contented" and "to know what to avoid." Laozi's philosophy of life is concerned with how to cultivate bodies and minds. Starting from the discourse on the relationship between man and external things, Laozi let people understand that compared with bodies and lives, external things are not worthy of note. He, then further explained that to achieve the harmony of the bodies and minds, the important thing is to lay more emphasis on the latter. Throughout *Laozi*, there are two concepts related to bodies and minds—"birth" and "body." The word "birth," which has two main connotations, appears most frequently. One is production, that is, from the mother, and the other one refers to life. Laozi said, "A formless entity existed prior to heaven and earth"; "Being is born from the nonbeing of Tao." There are also other concepts, such as "preserving lives," "striving for better lives" and "valuing lives" in *Laozi*.

Since the pre-Qin period, the Chinese people have been thinking that life is produced by the combination of shape and soul; moreover, in this combination, soul is the root while body or shape is only something that life depends on. Therefore, more importance is attached to soul than body. In Chapter 10, Laozi said, "Life is created by the combination of shape and soul. Shape and soul cannot be separated." But he also said, "It is not good to add some man-made elements to life" (Chapter 55), and "Doing nothing in life and letting it be outweigh regarding life as precious enough to be luxuriously self-indulgent" (Chapter 75).

In other words, Laozi's perspective on body and mind is actually a theory of health preservation. After distinguishing shape from soul and body from mind, he mainly attached importance to soul or mind, that is to say, the key to health preservation is to preserve mind and soul, returning people's spirit to "quietness" and their soul to "having no desires." This is called "being contented" and "knowing what to avoid." In this way, people can preserve their health and prolong their lives. Chapter 44 says,

A contented man will not be disgraced; a man who knows what to avoid will not be endangered. Such a man will stay safe forever.

There is a saying which goes like this, "Heart is loftier than the sky."

更何况普通人呢？概括地讲，老子的人生哲学的基本原则，就是要人依"大道"、"玄德"修身养性，依"大道"、"玄德"待人接物，就是要"知足"、"知止"。老子的人生哲学，是讨论如何修养身心的问题的。老子是先由讨论人与外物的关系开始，使人明白人和身体、生命相比，外物是不值得重视的；再进而说明要达到身体的和谐，最重要的是向内心用功。《老子》一书中与身心相关的是"生"和"身"两个概念。"生"字出现的次数很多，其含义主要有两个方面：一是产生，即由母体中生产出来；二是指生命。老子说："有物混成，先天地生"；"有生于无。"这些"生"字都是生产或产生的意思。《老子》中又有"摄生"、"益生"、"贵生"等概念，这其中的"生"字，都是指人的生命。

先秦以来的中国人都认为，生命是由形体与精神两部分结合而成；而且在这一结合体中，人的精神是根本，身体或形体只是生命的依托，因而这种认识具有某种精神重于肉体的倾向。老子既说："人的生命是由称为魄的形和称为魂的神结合而成的，形与神是不能分离的。"（第十章）但他同时又说："给生命人为地增加一些成分是不好的。"（第五十五章）"对生命无所作为、顺其自然，胜过把生命看得过分贵重而厚自奉养。"（第七十五章）

这也就是说，老子的身心观实际是一种养生理论，他对人的生命作了形神、身心的区分，强调人的神或心的重要性。就是说，人要养生，关键是要养神、养心，使人的精神归于"静"使人的心归于无欲。这叫"知足"和"知止"。这样，人就可以达到养生的目的，实现长生。《老子》第四十四章说：

知足不辱，知止不殆，可以长久。

俗话说："天不为高，只有人心才最高。"人的欲望是没有

Human desires are infinite. So, you must take good control of your desires. Taoist immortals of later ages asked people not to eat any of the five grains or to drink in order to become immortals. Unlike them, Laozi did not have this idea. Laozi had his own standard for what can be counted as "being contented" and "knowing what to avoid." Chapter 80 of *Laozi* says, "The people in a small country relish fine food, admire beautiful clothes, delight in traditional customs and relax in comfortable homes." This is his standard, which is also implied in what Zhuangzi said, "The mole drinks from the river, but only takes what fills its belly." In today's words, it is enough to solve the problem of food and clothing and other things are superfluous. Abiding by this standard is just "being contented" and "knowing what to avoid," which requires people to pursue subjectively rather than objectively. Therefore, Chapter 46 says,

> No crime is more severe than insatiable desire; no disaster is more tragic than discontent; no misfortune is more miserable than covetousness. Therefore, contented minds always have enough.

According to Laozi, the reason why people are not contented or have insatiable desires is, in terms of the theory of health preservation, that they do not realize which one is more important: body or mind, shape or soul, things or one's self, the internal or the external. Therefore, Chapter 13 says,

> Favor and disgrace trouble the mind; high rank and misfortune befall all mankind. How do favor and disgrace trouble the mind? Favor is no blessing: Winning it unsettles the mind with joy, losing it unsettles the mind with sorrow; consequently, favor and disgrace trouble the mind. How do high rank and misfortune befall all mankind? Misfortune befalls me because I have a body. If I have no body, how can it befall me?

Laozi's words here have caused much controversy in the past. One view is that the word "body" in the above passage refers to one's self and the individual is asked to forget himself and regard himself as the root of evil. Another view is that the word "body" refers to one's physical body and it is also equivalent to life. The reason why misfortune befalls all men is that they all have the bodies. However, now that life has come into being, it should be preserved and cherished well. Sima Guang, a great historian of the Northern Song Dynasty, said, "Misfortune befalls us if we have bodies. But since we have bodies, we should honor and cherish them, comply with the laws of nature to handle things and do not indulge our passions, so as to free them from misfortune." The theory of "loving bodies" was thus derived.

止境的。所以，一定要控制好你的欲望。当然，老子和后来的道教神仙家并不相同，他没有叫人不食五谷（即"辟谷"），没有叫人不吃不喝以追求成仙。老子没有这个主张。对怎样才算"知足"、"知止"，老子有他的标准。《老子》第八十章说："小国"里的人民"甘其食，美其服，安其居，乐其俗"。这就是他的标准。庄子说："偃鼠在河中饮水，不过喝饱肚子而已。"说的也是这个意思。按今天的话说，就是解决温饱就够了，其他都是多余的。遵守这个标准，就是"知足"、"知止"。这是叫人向主观寻求，而不应向客观外物寻求。所以，《老子》第四十六章说：

> 罪莫大于可欲，祸莫大于不知足，咎莫大于欲得。故
> 知足之足，恒足矣。

老子认为，人们之所以不知足，贪欲那么多，从养生的理论来说，是因为他没有分清身心、形神、物我、外内之间，孰轻孰重。《老子》第十三章说：

> 宠辱若惊，贵大患若身。何谓宠辱若惊？宠为下，得
> 之若惊，失之若惊，是谓宠辱若惊。何谓贵大患若身？
> 吾所以有大患者，为吾有身，及吾无身，吾有何患？

老子的这段话，以往引起了很大的争论。一种观点认为，文中的"身"，就是指自身、自己。老子这里是叫人忘掉自身、忘掉自己，是把自身、自己视为祸患的根源。另一种看法认为，《老子》文中的"身"是指身体，也相当于生命，是说人之所以有祸患，就因为有这么个身体的存在；但生命既然已经形成，就应该好好地保养、爱护它。北宋的大历史学家司马光说："有我们的身体就会有祸患。但既然已有了这个身体，就应该使它尊贵、爱护它，顺应自然规律，来应对事物，不放纵情欲，使它没有祸患。"于是从中引出了"贵身"的理论。

Both of the views are reasonable, but neither of them is totally correct. As a matter of fact, the word "body" here refers not only to one's self, but also to one's physical body. Laozi just asked people to look at things from different angles. People should be aware that man is more important than external things, that a human being is the duality of shape and soul or body and mind, and that the real solution to the problem should be found from one's mind. In terms of the relationship between favor or disgrace and one's body or life, both favor and disgrace belong to the external things; only your body and life belong to you, which really need to be valued and cherished. In this sense, Laozi did not deny body or life; instead, he stood for "valuing lives" or "loving bodies."

However, "valuing lives" or "loving bodies" does not mean small favors or "love" in general that one continually gives oneself; instead, one should be "void," "simple" and "do nothing" like "Tao" and "virtue." In other words, "Heaven and earth are inhumane, indifferent to everything like worthless straw-dog sacrifices; the sage is inhumane, indifferent to everyone like worthless straw-dog sacrifices." In this sense, "no bodies" should be emphasized in "health preservation," that is, one's self should be forgotten. Thus, Chapter 7 says,

Heaven is enduring and earth is everlasting. Heaven and earth enjoy longevity— their selflessness gives them longevity. Therefore, the sage withdraws but still shines forth; he excludes himself and thus is saved. Isn't it because of his selflessness that he has attained his purposes?

It is on account of this that Laozi stood for "no bodies" and forgetting oneself rather than " striving for a better life," "desiring to hold on to life" or "abundant means of sustentation." Chapter 50 says,

From the cradle to the grave, three in ten will live a full life cycle, three in ten will die prematurely, three in ten are always at death's door. Why are they always at death's door? It is because they desire to hold on to life.

As a result, Laozi clearly stated, "To strive for a better life is ill-advised" and "The sage rejects extremes, excesses, and extravagance" (Chapter 29).

Why is "to strive for a better life" ill-advised? It should be also seen from two aspects. From the perspective of the relationship between man and external things, "striving for a better life" is in name for the care of body and life, but in fact it reverses the subject-object relationship. If one attaches

这两种看法都有道理，但又都不完全正确。其实，老子这里的"身"，既指自身、自己，也指身体、形体。老子是叫人从多方面看问题，既要看到在人与外物之间，人是最重要的；还要看到人是形神、身心的二元结合，要从人的内心来寻找真正能解决问题的途径。从荣辱与人的身体、生命的关系来看，荣也好，辱也好，都是外在之物，只有你自己的身体、你的生命才是你自己的，才真正需要珍惜、爱护。从这个意义上讲，老子不是否定身体，更不是否定生命，而是主张"贵生"或"贵身"。

但是，"贵生"或"贵身"，又不是常人眼中给自己不断施与小恩小惠的"爱"，而是如"道"、"德"那样"虚"、"朴"、"无为"。即所谓"天地不仁，以万物为刍狗；圣人不仁，以百姓为刍狗。"从这个意义上讲，"养生"又应该强调"无身"，从心中忘掉自身。《老子》第七章说：

> 天长地久。天地所以能长且久者，以其不自生，故能长久。是以圣人后其身而身先，外其身而身存。非以其无私邪？故能成其私。

正是因为这个原因，老子主张"无身"、忘掉自身，而反对"益生"、"生生之厚"或"厚生"。《老子》第五十章说：

> 出生入死。生之徒十有三，死之徒十有三，人之生，动于死地亦十有三。夫何故？以其生生之厚。

所以，老子明确地说："益生是不祥之举。"圣人要"去甚，去奢，去泰"（第二十九章），即去掉一切超出了正常限度的过分养护。

为什么说"益生是不祥之举"呢？这也要从两个方面来看。从人与外物的关系这个角度来看，"益生"虽然名义上是为了爱护身体、奉养生命，但实际上则颠倒了主客关系。如果把功

excessive importance to the external things, such as rank, fame, fortune, sensual pleasure and rich food and believes that doing so can benefit his life, these things will only become burdens, injuring his body and life. At least he misplaces body or life and the external things. So, Chapter 44 says,

Which is more precious, your name or life? Which is more valuable, your life or wealth? Which is more harmful, your gains or losses?

According to Laozi, fame, possessions, gains and losses are all trivial compared with body and life. He who really understands health preservation loves himself more than anything else. This is also implied in what Zhuangzi said, "The true object of the mighty Tao is the preservation of the body. Quite subordinate to this is its use in the management of the state, while the dust onto the ground is used in the government of the world." ❶ It also means that, in terms of health preservation, only life and body are important.

From another perspective, Laozi thought that knowing the importance of body and life is just the beginning of health preservation. What and how to preserve is the question. Life is the wonderful combination of shape and soul or body and mind, so what they preserve and what they preserve first are still questions. Taoism holds that soul is the root, which depends on shape. Therefore, Laozi thought that health preservation should not be limited to supporting the body, eating and drinking extravagantly or indulging in sensual pleasure to satisfy the appetite. Thus, Chapter 12 says,

The five colors can blind the eye; the five tastes can dull the palate; the five tones can deafen the ear; chasing and hunting can madden the mind; rare goods can lure the heart.

The so-called "five colors," "five tones," "five tastes," "chasing and hunting" and "rare goods" are, in simple words, beautiful things, melodious sounds, delicious food, interesting activities and valuable goods. But Laozi denied all these things, saying that they do people no good because they not only injure people's bodies, but also disrupt their minds and damage the root of life.

Some people are skeptical about his opinion. It is because Laozi once

名利禄、声色厚味这些身外之物看得过重，认为只有这样才会有益于生命，这些恰恰会成为生命的负担，残害了身体，损伤了生命，至少是把身体或生命与外物的位置摆错了。《老子》第四十四章说：

> 名与身孰亲？身与货孰多？得与亡孰病？

老子认为，名利、财产、得失与自己的身体、生命相比，都是微不足道的。真正懂得养生的人，爱自己胜过爱任何东西。庄子说："大道的真精神用来保养自身，剩余下来的部分用来治理国家，掉到地上的渣滓就用来治理天下。"❶ 这也说明，对养生而言，只有生命、身体，才是最重要的。

从另一个方面来看，老子认为，一个人懂得了身体、生命才是真正重要的，这还只是养生的开始，还有一个养什么和如何养的问题。因为人的生命是形神、身心二元的巧妙结合，那这两部分养什么不养什么，先养什么后养什么，都是问题。道家认为，在形神之间神是根本，形是依托。所以，老子也认为养生不应该只是供养形体，山吃海喝，满足口腹之欲、纵情声色。《老子》第十二章说：

> 五色令人目盲，五音令人耳聋，五味令人口爽，驰骋
> 田猎令人心发狂，难得之货令人行妨。

所谓"五色"、"五音"、"五味"、"驰骋田猎"、"难得之货"，通俗地讲，就是好看的、好听的、好吃的、好玩的和贵重的东西。对这些老子一概加以否定，说这些东西对人没有一点好处，因为它们不仅损伤了人的身体，而且还扰乱了人的心神，动摇了人的生命的根本。

有人对老子的这个观点产生了疑问。因为老子曾是主张圣

---

❶《庄子·让王》。

❶ "Rangwang," *Zhuangzi.*

maintained that the sage should not only be "as ignorant as a fool," but also "keep the people in the dark" and "empty their minds and fill their stomachs." Now, isn't it good that people are all in pursuit of rich food and sensual pleasure? Why does he reject it? As a matter of fact, it is a misunderstanding. Laozi's proposition is directed against chaos, strife, mutual suspicion and deception, tactics and adroitness, and people are expected to be contented, know what to avoid and return to nature, rather than beat their brains out to harm others and themselves. According to him, if people are like this, they will naturally require the low living standards only lest they should indulge in fantasies and make trouble when they do not worry about food and clothes. However, the progress of the society will not stop. In addition, Laozi did not simply expose and criticize the ugly phenomena in the realistic society; instead, he further explained that excessive sensual pleasure for the people with low living standards can even be harmful. Transcending the "fool" stage of attending to stomachs, people are under the impression that they have come to the "knowledge" stage, which can meet the need of life to the utmost. After that, they should again return to the "fool" stage, giving up the excessive sensual pleasure of their own accord. However, the latter "fool" with the meaning of "great wisdom appearing slow-witted" is different from the first "fool." Laozi was opposed to "the five colors," "the five tones," "the five tastes," "chasing and hunting" and "rare goods." According to him, in pursuing these things, people only take into consideration the preservation of their bodies while ignoring or even harming their minds. Thus, they will take the old road of "abundant means of sustentation." However, Laozi's theory of health preservation involves that between shape and soul or body and mind, more importance should be attached to soul and mind, which is "deep-rootedness, the way of long life and eternal vision." If a person's soul and mind are preserved well and he "is contented" and "knows what to avoid," he will naturally attain the harmony of shape and soul and the harmony of body and mind—it is also the basic purpose of health preservation.

Besides this principle of health preservation, the theory also puts forward many specific methods, such as "being as pure as undyed silk and as simple as uncarved wood" and "emptying yourself of everything and letting the mind be at peace." Laozi said, "The ancient sages who were followers of Tao... simple, like an uncarved block of wood" (Chapter 15); "He who is overflowing with virtue will return to the simple state of uncarved wood" (Chapter 28); "If desire arises in this process, let it be stifled with the nameless Tao" (Chapter 37). All these imply that one must "be as pure as undyed silk and as simple as uncarved

人应追求"愚人之心"的，并且要使老百姓"愚之"，要"虚其心，实其腹"。现在人民都去追求口腹之欲和声色犬马之乐了，这不是很好吗？为什么又要去反对呢？其实这是误解。老子说的"愚人之心"和要使百姓"愚之"，那是针对天下的混乱纷争、尔虞我诈、权谋机巧而言的，是要人们知足知止，返璞归真，不要为害人害己的事费脑筋了。老子认为人如果这样，自然就只要求满足很低层次的生活标准了；就可以衣食无忧之后，不去胡思乱想，惹事生非了。但是，社会不会停止进步，老子也不只是简单地揭露和批判现实生活中的种种丑恶现象，而是进一步说明，即使是满足低层次的口腹之乐，过分了也是有害的。人应该在超越了最初"为腹"的"愚"阶段，自认为进入到了能极度满足生活需要的"知"的阶段之后，再次向"愚"回归，主动舍弃过分的口腹声色之乐。但这一次的"愚"和上次的"愚"不一样了，这一次是"大智若愚"。可以说，老子反对"五色"、"五音"、"五味"、"驰骋田猎"和"难得之货"，主要是认为追求这些，只考虑到了奉养人的形体，会忽视甚至伤害到人的心神，走上了"厚生"的老路。而老子的养生理论认为，在形神、身心之间，更应重视精神和心性，这才是"深根固柢，长生久视之道"。如果一个人的心、神安养好了，懂得了"知足"、"知止"，那自然就可以达到形神与身心的和谐了——这才是人养生的根本目的。

　　除了这一养生的基本原则之外，老子的养生理论还提出了许多具体的方法。如见素抱朴、致虚守静等等。老子说："古之善为道者……敦兮其若朴"（第十五章）；"常德乃足，复归于朴"（第二十八章）；"化而欲作，吾将镇之以无名之朴"

wood" in character cultivation and health preservation.

Then, to what degree can one be counted as "being as pure as undyed silk and as simple as uncarved wood, diminishing his selfishness and reducing his desire" ? Is there any example of such personality for us to rate ourselves?

Laozi cites two examples: One is the sage and the other is the newly-born baby.

The "sage" "follows Tao alone," so it is unquestionable for him to "be as pure as undyed silk and as simple as uncarved wood, to diminish his selfishness and reduce his desire." Unfortunately, the "sage" does not live together with the common people so that they cannot follow his example. However, this is not the case with the newly-born baby. Growing up from a baby, everyone should have some memories about his babyhood; moreover, newly-born babies can be easily seen everywhere so that it is quite easy for the common people to notice their voices and expressions. Thus, Laozi often used a newly-born baby as an example to show how a person can be "pure," "simple" and can "diminish his selfishness and reduce his desire." For example, Laozi said, "Can you control your breath like a supple newly-born baby?" (Chapter 10) "Like a newly-born baby who has not yet learned to smile" (Chapter 20); "He who is endowed with eternal virtue will return to the natural state of a newly-born baby" (Chapter 28). Chapter 55 says again,

> A man of high virtue is like a newly-born baby. Wasps, scorpions, and poisonous snakes will not hurt him; wild beasts and birds of prey will not attack him. While his bones are weak and his sinews tender, his grip is firm. Having never experienced sexual union, he is still fully aroused: He has attained manhood's full measure. Screaming all day, he never becomes hoarse: He has achieved perfect equilibrium.

Emptying yourself of everything and letting the mind be at peace is also another specific method of health preservation and character cultivation. Chapter 16 says,

> Empty yourself of everything and let the mind be at peace. When all things are growing, I observe their regeneration. Anything and everything returns to its source, which is called "peace of mind." Peace of mind means returning to nature.

"Emptying yourself of everything" is linked with "Tao," while "peace" is linked with "mystical virtue." What is implied in these sentences is that people who preserve their health and cultivate their character should be as modest as "the mighty Tao" and as quiet as "mystical virtue." They should

（第三十七章）都是说修身、养生，必须要"见素抱朴"。

那么，一个人在养生、修身养性方面要达到什么样子，才算是做到了"见素抱朴，少私寡欲"了呢？有没有一个人格的标本，以便我们去对照呢？

老子树立了两个榜样：一个是圣人，另一个就是婴儿。

"圣人""惟道是从"，能做到"见素抱朴，少私寡欲"那是不用怀疑的。只是"圣人"并不和平常人生活在一起，普通人无法照着这个榜样去做。但婴儿却不一样。每个人都由婴儿长成，都应留有一些关于婴儿的记忆，而且自己身边也不缺少婴儿，他们的音容笑貌很容易观察到。所以，老子常常用婴儿为例，说明人如何才是"朴"、"素"，才是"少私寡欲"。如老子说："专气致柔，能婴儿乎？"（第十章）"沌沌兮，如婴儿之未孩。"（第二十章）"常德不离，复归于婴儿。"（第二十八章）这些就都是以婴儿为榜样的。《老子》第五十五章又说：

> 含德之厚，比于赤子。毒虫不螫，猛兽不据，攫鸟不搏。骨弱筋柔而握固。未知牝牡之合而朘作，精之至也。终日号而不嗄，和之至也。

致虚守静，也是老子提出的一条养生和修身的具体方法。《老子》第十六章说：

> 致虚极，守静笃，万物并作，吾以观复。夫物芸芸，各复归其根。归根曰静，是谓复命。

这里的"虚极"是指"道"而言，"静笃"即是极端地"静"，应指"玄德"而言。这几句的意思是说，养生、修身的人，应该如"大道"那样虚心，如"玄德"那样寂静，从万物

observe, from the growth of all things, the law that "reversion is the way of 'Tao.'" The numerous and complicated things in the world will finally return to their root—"emptying themselves of everything and letting the minds be at peace"—and to their nature respectively. According to Laozi, the sea is the king of countless streams because it lies below them; female animals are better than male ones by "emptying themselves of everything and letting their minds be at peace." Therefore, he came to the conclusion that "heaven takes precedence over lightness; calmness rules over hastiness" (Chapter 26); "the loftiest virtue seems humble; the amplest virtue seems deficient" (Chapter 41); and "exertion and agitation overcome cold; tranquility and calmness overcome heat. He who is quiet and still will rule over the world" (Chapter 45). "Emptying yourself of everything and letting the mind be at peace" can return to nature and be as everlasting as "the mighty Tao" and "mystical virtue."

Of course, *Laozi* also talked about some specific principles and ways of life, such as "being humble and not competing with others," "having good intentions toward others" and "retiring after success," which are in fact just the specification of philosophical thought of "being contented" and "knowing what to avoid."

2. Achieving Perfect Equilibrium

With the wisdom of a philosopher and from the theoretical level of "Tao" and "virtue," Laozi expounded on how to cultivate character and preserve health, the principles and ways of life, which can give us a lot of enlightenments. But many of his principles and methods, such as "being humble and not competing with others," "having good intentions toward others," "retiring after success" and "being quiet and doing nothing," are usually misunderstood as a kind of flexible tactics or strategies. It is also misunderstood that "selflessness" advocated by him is actually a means of realizing selfishness.

We hold that these viewpoints are just misreadings of Laozi. To grasp his philosophy of life, including the specific principles and methods about the relationship between body and mind, the individual and others, two points must be paid attention to: One is the starting point and the other is the purpose and destination.

In view of the starting point of his philosophy of life, Laozi is different from other philosophers. Instead of taking stop-gap measures, he kept his eyes on the future, nipping problems in the bud, which is similar to "preventive treatment of disease" in traditional Chinese medical science. This is implied in

动作生长的过程中，观察到"反者道之动"的规律。世上的事物纷繁复杂，最终都要返回到它们的本根，即处虚守静，这就是复归各自的本性。老子认为，江海都虚怀处下，故能为百川之王；动物雌性总是以持虚守静而胜于雄性。所以，他得出结论："重为轻根，静为躁君。"（第二十六章）"上德若谷"，"广德若不足。"（第四十一章）"躁胜寒，静胜热，清静为天下正。"（第四十五章）致虚守静，可返本归真，和"大道"、"玄德"一样地长久。

当然，《老子》中还讲了一些很具体的处世原则和方法，如贵柔守雌、挫锐解纷、和光同尘、谦虚不争、与人为善、功成身退等等，但这些实际上只是"知足"、"知止"哲学思想的具体化。

（二）和之至也

老子以哲人的智慧，从"道"、"德"的高度，论述了一个人应该如何修身、养生及待人处世的原则和方法，能给我们很多启发。但老子的许多原则和方法，如谦柔不争、致虚守静、功遂身退、清静无为等等，常常被人误解为一种权谋，一种策略，认为老子所宣扬的"无私"，其实只是实现自私的手段。

我们认为，这些看法是对老子的误读。把握老子的人生哲学，包括他所提出的处理个人身心和个人与他人关系的具体原则和方法，必须注意两个方面：一是出发点，二是其目的与归宿。

从老子人生哲学的出发点来看，老子与其他哲学家不同，他不是针对人生具体问题提出头痛医头、脚痛医脚的方案，而是着眼于未来、防患于未然，就像中医所说的"治未病"。即在你身体还没有生病前加强养生，进行预防。《老子》第六十

Chapter 63,

Tackle hard tasks while they are still easy; tend to complicated affairs while they are simple. Solve a difficult problem by attacking its weakest link; accomplish a great deed by attending to small details. The sage never attempts to do great deeds; in this way, he succeeds.

In Chapter 64, Laozi further summarized this law,

Order is easy to sustain before disorder arises; trouble is easy to stop before it starts; fragile objects are easy to shatter; small items are easy to scatter; tackle a problem before it begins; set things in order before they unravel. A huge tree grows from one tiny shoot; a towering terrace begins with one basket of earth; a journey of a thousand miles begins with one small step.

Laozi also listed specific examples to show that the starting point of his philosophy of life is out of the ordinary. Chapter 79 says,

When a bitter hatred is resolved, some resentment lingers; how is this satisfying? The sage keeps his contract and never demands his due.

In view of the destination of his philosophy of life, the "selfishness" he wanted to accomplish is not "selfishness" concerning name and gain in general but a very important category in the ancient Chinese philosophy. Actually, it is "equilibrium," a very high realm of life.

"Equilibrium" is originally a concept used to describe the resonance of sound. Laozi also said that echo and sound are two expressions of resonance. This is the original meaning of "equilibrium." Nevertheless, Laozi not only advocated and pursued "equilibrium" when he talked about "sound," but also applied "equilibrium" to his discussion on health preservation and conducting himself in society. He even extended it to his whole philosophy of life. It can be said that advocating and pursuing "equilibrium" is the highest aim and realm of his philosophy of life.

Laozi said that the ultimate accomplishment in self-cultivation is to attain a newborn baby's virtue: "Screaming all day, he never becomes hoarse: He has achieved perfect equilibrium." This is the "equilibrium" in his theory of health preservation.

三章说：

> 图难于其易，为大于其细。天下之难作于易，天下之大作于细。是以圣人终不为大，故能成其大。

第六十四章，老子进一步总结这一规律说：

> 其安易持，其未兆易谋，其脆易泮，其微易散。为之于未有，治之于未乱。合抱之木，生于毫末；九层之台，起于垒土；千里之行，始于足下。

老子还举出具体事例，来说明他的人生哲学的出发点是与众不同的。《老子》第七十九章说：

> 和大怨，必有余怨，安可以为善？是以圣人执左契，而不责于人。

从老子人生哲学的归宿来看，老子所要成就的"私"，不是一般私名私利之"私"，而实际是中国古代哲学的一个重要范畴、一种非常高的人生境界——"和"。

"和"，本是一个形容声音相应、和谐的概念，老子也有"音声相和"之说。这是"和"字的本义。但老子不仅在谈论"音声"时主张"和"，追求"和"；他还将"和"用于谈论人的养生、处世，扩展到他的整个人生哲学。可以说，主张"和"、追求"和"，是老子人生哲学的最高目标与境界。

老子曾经说，人生的修养最终是要达到像婴儿般的品德："终日号而不嗄，和之至也。"这是老子养生论上的"和"。

According to Laozi, a person should not make a showy display of his abilities so as not to hurt others, and should get rid of all kinds of disputes, and "conceal his brilliance and be as humble as dust." Even if one has a bitter hatred, he should resolve it of his own accord. It is obvious that "equilibrium" is also the aim of his philosophy of conducting oneself in society.

Some specific principles and methods of his philosophy of life, such as "being as pure as undyed silk and as simple as uncarved wood," "emptying yourself of everything and letting the mind be at peace," "doing nothing and not competing with others," "retiring after success" and "having good intentions toward others," are aimed at one word—"equilibrium." The ultimate goal and the highest realm of Laozi's philosophy of life are to realize the harmony between body and mind, shape and soul, oneself and others and finally the harmony of the whole society. Chapter 55 says, "Equilibrium signifies accord with the natural way; to know this natural way is to be filled with insight." Wang Bi annotated, "All things depend on equilibrium for the natural way, so to know equilibrium is to attain it." Laozi referred to "the mighty Tao" as "the eternal Tao" and regarded "embracing Tao" and "attaining Tao" as the ultimate goal. In other words, attaining the harmonious realm is regarded as the highest purpose of life.

　　老子又说，人生在世，应该磨去你的锋芒，以免刺伤他人；解除各种纷争，"和其光，同其尘"。即是说，你虽光泽照人，却不耀人眼目。他还说，即使与人有大怨，也要主动去和解，这叫"和大怨"。可见，老子处世哲学的宗旨也是"和"。

　　老子的人生哲学的一些具体原则和方法，无论见素抱朴、致虚守静也好，无为不争、谦柔退让、与人为善也好，都是为了一个"和"字。实现个人身心、形神的和谐，实现自己与他人之间的和谐，并最终实现整个社会的和谐。这是老子人生哲学的最终目标和最高境界。《老子》第五十五章说："知和曰常，知常曰明。"王弼的注释说："物以和为常，故知和则得常也。"老子称"大道"为"常（恒）道"，以"同于道"和"得道"为最终目标，也就是以实现和谐境界为人生的最高目标。

十七世纪画家石涛的作品，渗透着老子阴阳虚实的美学理念

Drawing of Shi Tao in the 17th century, saturating with Laozi's aesthetic view of *Yin* and *Yang*

七　唯美与恶，相去若何

——老子的美学思想

Chapter Ⅶ　　Is There a Difference Between Good and Evil?

　　　　　　　　　　—Laozi's Aesthetic Thought

Aesthetics is the study of beauty. It focuses on a series of theoretical problems concerning what is beauty and how human beings create and appreciate beauty. Laozi did not deal with such aesthetic problems theoretically. Neither was beauty the chief concern of his aesthetic thought. However, *Laozi* did set forth what is "beauty," discuss how to judge beauty and advance some important aesthetic categories and propositions. Since Laozi was born earlier than Confucius who sought advice from Laozi, we may conclude that as the first philosopher and esthetician in China, Laozi started the study of aesthetics in China.

1. Beauty as Beauty

What is Laozi's view of beauty? It is mentioned in Chapter 2 of *Laozi*,

When everyone knows beauty as beauty, ugliness is revealed; when everyone knows goodness as goodness, evil is revealed. Being and nonbeing are two phases of existence; difficult and easy are two stages of persistence; long and short are two degrees of distance; high and low are two ranks of eminence; echo and sound are two expressions of resonance; before and after are two orders of sequence.

Beauty here bears the meaning of good looks in terms of one's physical appearance, whereas evil means ugliness.

Although beauty is not clearly defined in his words, Laozi did mention "beauty" and how to treat beauty. According to him, "beauty" differs from "goodness." The Chinese character for "evil" consists of two word elements, "inferior" and "heart." The word "inferior" is the ancient form of "evil" today. In *Explanatory Notes to Chinese Characters*, the first Chinese dictionary, the character denoting "inferior" was interpreted as "ugly, like an arched back." It was seen as a pictographic character, in the shape of a humpback. Therefore, in Chinese, the original meaning of "evil" is ugly. Since beauty is opposed to evil, and the latter means ugly, then it is evident that beauty bears the meaning of good-looking and pretty physical appearance. In *Explanatory Notes to Chinese Characters*, "good" means "auspicious." Laozi distinguished beauty from

美学，就是关于美的学问。它主要是研究什么是美，人如何进行审美创造和审美鉴赏等一系列理论问题。老子并没有对上述美学问题进行过专门的理论探讨，甚至老子美学思想中最重要的范畴也不是"美"。但《老子》一书中却涉及到什么是"美"、人应该如何审美等重要的美学问题，并提出一些重要的美学范畴与命题。因为老子的生年略早于孔子，而且孔子曾经求教于老子。所以，我们可以说，一部中国美学史实际是从老子那里开始的，老子是中国历史上第一位哲学思想家，也是中国历史上第一位美学家。

（一）美之为美

老子是如何看待"美"的呢？《老子》第二章说：

> 天下皆知美之为美，斯恶已；皆知善之为善，斯不善也。故有无相生，难易相成，长短相形，高下相倾，音声相和，前后相随。

这段话中的"美"是"好"的意思，指人的相貌美、漂亮；"恶"是"丑"的意思。

在这段话中，老子并没有明确告诉我们什么是"美"。但老子在这段话中的确谈到了"美"，并且还谈到了怎样看待"美"。老子认为，"美"与"善"是不同的。"恶"字由"亚"和"心"构成，"亚"与"恶"字是古今字，即"亚"是"恶"的本字。中国历史上第一部字典《说文解字》给"亚"的解释是："亚，丑也。象人局背之形。"这是把"亚"解释成一个象形字，说它像人驼背的形状。所以"恶"的本义就是丑、难看的意思。"美"与"恶"相对，"恶"既指人的长相丑、难看，"美"自然就是指人的长相好看、漂亮了。《说文解字》解释"善"的意思是"吉也"，即好、吉利的意思。老子正是着眼于

goodness. He defined beauty by means of senses, while goodness in terms of moral values. *Laozi* was the first one to make a clear demarcation between the two words, for no one had ever done it before him. The word "goodness" was frequently used in *Laozi*, but all were from the angle of rational judgment by moral values with no exception. The use of "beauty" is threefold, contrary to "evil" in meaning (ugly) as in Chapter 2 and 20, in combination with "words" as in Chapter 62 and 81, or used as a verb, describing one's psychological reaction to one's clothes, as in "admire beautiful clothes" in Chapter 80. No matter in what context, the word is used to describe whether one's physical appearance is good or not, whether one's words are pleasing to the ear, or whether one is pleased with his clothes. All these usages prove that Laozi used the word from the angle of senses. In his eyes, "beauty" brings happiness or comfort to the senses of sight or hearing, whereas "goodness" is an abstract virtue, based on rational judgment.

Another characteristic of Laozi's understanding of "beauty" lies in his use of the word in contrast with "ugliness." The meaning of the word is clarified in the unity of opposites. "When everyone knows beauty as beauty, ugliness is revealed; when everyone knows goodness as goodness, evil is revealed. Being and nonbeing are two phases of existence; difficult and easy are two stages of persistence; long and short are two degrees of distance; high and low are two ranks of eminence; echo and sound are two expressions of resonance; before and after are two orders of sequence." All these opposites, beauty and ugliness, goodness and evil, being and nonbeing, difficult and easy, long and short, high and low, echo and sound, before and after, are paradoxical, yet interdependent and unified. This is the paradox theory. Without evil, goodness is nowhere to find; without nonbeing, being cannot exist. Likewise, there is no beauty without ugliness. In Chapter 11 of *Laozi*, the paradoxical theory is illustrated with the example of being and nonbeing,

> Thirty spokes share the hub of a wheel; the hub is useful because of
> the space within. Clay is kneaded to mold a vessel; the vessel is useful

人的感官来论美、丑的。这就把"美"与着眼于道德价值的"善"完全区别开来了。在老子之前，"美"的概念已经开始与"善"的概念分离，但还没有被人明确地加以区别，老子是明确区别"美"与"善"的第一人。《老子》一书中使用"善"概念的地方很多，但无一例外地都是在道德价值评判的层面上使用的；而"美"的概念，一是在与"恶"（即"丑"）相对的意义上使用（第二章、第二十章），二是在与"言"组合为"美言"一词时使用（第六十二章、第八十一章），三是在形容人的服饰所引起的心理反应时，作为动词使用，即"美其服"（第八十章）。这三种情况，或着眼于人的长相好看，或着眼于人的言词漂亮、动听，或着眼于人穿着美丽、鲜艳的服饰时心里的美感或精神的愉悦，都说明老子是从人的感官上来考察"美"的性质的。在他的眼中，"美"应该是那些能给人的视觉、听觉等感官带来快感与舒适的东西，而"善"则是一种抽象的品德，是一种基于理性的判断。

老子论"美"的另一个特点是，老子总是把"美"放在与"丑"相对之中，在"美"与"丑"的对立统一之中来说明"美"是什么的。所谓"天下皆知美之为美，斯恶已；皆知善之为善，斯不善已。故有无相生，难易相成，长短相形，高下相倾，音声相和，前后相随。"就是说，美与丑、善与恶、有与无、难与易、长与短、高与下、音与声、前与后，这些矛盾的对立面，既是互相对立和排斥的，又是互相依存、互相统一的。这就是相反相成的道理。离开了"恶"就无所谓"善"；离开了"无"就无谓"有"。同样，离开了"丑"也就无所谓"美"。《老子》第十一章以"有"、"无"为例，阐述矛盾对立的这种互相依存、互相统一的关系说：

　　三十辐共一毂，当其无，有车之用。埏埴以为器，当

because of the space within. Doors and windows are cut from the walls of a room; the room is useful because of the space within.

This shows that though the opposites are paradoxical, they are correlative and interdependent. They exist on the premise of the existence of the opposite, with which they are in unity. Moreover, they are in gradual transformation into each other. Those previously big, superior, before, living, positive, hard, auspicious, etc., may become the later small, inferior, after, dead, negative, soft, ominous, etc. Laozi said, "Good fortune contains bad fortune; bad fortune conceals good fortune. Who knows why?" (Chapter 58) "Maturity is followed by decline" (Chapter 55); "A strong army may fail in its attacks; a hard tree is ready for the axe" (Chapter 76). What is implied in these words is the universal law of "Reversion is the way of Tao." Similarly, "beauty" and "ugliness" are not invariable. Beauty may become plain, even ugly; ugliness may become plain, even beautiful. In this case, the boundary between "beauty" and "ugliness" becomes vague. In Chapter 20, Laozi said,

Is there a difference between yes and no? Is there a difference between good and evil?

The original Chinese character for "no" bears the meaning of "flattery," yet the word for "no" in the Transcript "A" of the Silk-Book *Laozi* means "abuse." Some famous modern scholars, including Liu Shipei, are of the opinion that the word should be "abuse." The Chinese character for "yes" in the above words connotes saying "yes" while nodding consent, or being absolutely obedient. In *Explanatory Notes to Chinese Characters*, the character denoting "abuse" was interpreted as "abuse, reproach out of rage." Wang Bi annotated, "Yes and no, good and evil, what is the difference?" This proves that the antonym to "yes" should be "abuse," not "flattery." In his words, Laozi intended to convey the idea that there is scarcely any difference between yes and no. What is the difference between good and evil? According to Laozi, there is no clear boundary between them, and both are likely to become the opposite side under certain circumstances.

Then, in Laozi's view, is there anything that can be regarded as the genuine "beauty?" Or what does the genuine and absolute "beauty" look like in his thought?

In general, "beauty" is connected with those items that bring pleasantness to people's senses of sight and hearing, such as bright colors

其无，有器之用。凿户牖以为室，当其无，有室之用。

这说明，矛盾的双方不仅是互相对立的，也是相互联系、相互依存的，各以自己的对立面作为自己存在的前提，同处于一个统一体中。而且，矛盾的双方还是处于不断向对立面转化的过程之中的。那些过去大的、高的、前的、生的、正的、刚的、吉的……将来都有可能变成为小的、下的、后的、死的、反的、柔的、凶的……。老子说："祸兮，福之所倚；福兮，祸之所伏。孰知其极？"（第五十八章）"物壮则老。"（第五十五章）"兵强则灭，木强则折。"（第七十六章）说的都是"反者道之动"这一矛盾运动的普遍规律。同样，"美"与"恶"（丑）也不是一成不变的。美也可以变得不美甚至丑；丑也可以变得不丑甚至美。这时"美"和"恶"（丑）的界限，似乎又变得模糊起来了。《老子》第二十章说：

唯之与阿，相去几何？美之与恶，相去若何？

"唯之与阿"一句中的"阿"字，帛书《老子》甲本作"诃"。近代著名学者刘师培等人也认为应该作"诃"。"唯"，是点头称是的答应声，即唯唯诺诺。"诃"《说文解字》说："诃，大言而怒也。"王弼的注释说："唯诃、美恶，相去若何。"也正说明与"唯"相对的是"诃"，不是"阿"。老子这段话的意思是说，奉承唯诺与违忤怒斥，这两者之间有多少差别呢？美的和丑的这两者之间又有多大距离呢？老子认为，这两者之间是没有什么绝对的界限的；在一定的条件下，两者都会走向自己的反面。

那么，在老子那里，有没有什么东西是真正的"美"呢？或者说，在老子的思想中，真正的、绝对的"美"是什么样的呢？

一般说来，"美"应该是那些能给人的视觉、听觉等感官

and pleasing sounds. These are visible and tangible. Laozi's dialectical thoughts can be seen everywhere. Chapter 45 reads, "Complete perfection seems flawed;" "Brimming fullness seems empty;" "Absolute straightness seems crooked; sheer cleverness seems awkward; supreme eloquence seems mute." The perfect image of beauty in Laozi's aesthetic thought, or the absolutely "beautiful" sample, should be the invisible and intangible Tao, the root of everything on earth and the supreme entity. Chapter 41 of *Laozi* says,

> An enormous square seems to have no corners; a massive vessel seems ever incomplete; a thunderous sound seems mute; an immense image seems shapeless; the glorified Tao seems indefinable.

Since Tao is everywhere and inside everything, it is too invisible and formless to be specified. If people are to depict it, it is like what Laozi wrote in Chapter 35, "The taste of Tao is insipid; the sight of Tao is invisible; the sound of Tao is inaudible; the use of Tao is inexhaustible." It is the end, the finality. From this aspect, Laozi's "Tao" is the " most admirable beauty" ❶ implied by Zhuangzi in the statement, "Heaven and earth proceed in the most admirable way, but they say nothing about them." In Laozi's eyes, the beauty recognized by common people, such as "the five tones, five colors, and flowery words," is vulgar, small and inferior. "Once Tao is lost, virtue arises; once virtue is lost, humaneness arises; once humaneness is lost, righteousness arises; once righteousness is lost, propriety arises." Not only did Laozi deny it, he also made a pointed critique, "The five colors can blind the eye; the five tones can deafen the ear; the five tastes can dull the palate; chasing and hunting can madden the mind; rare goods can lure the heart" (Chapter 12).

Laozi distinguished "beauty" and beautiful artistic works, and classified them into "the most admirable beauty," "the superior beauty," and "the least admirable beauty," "the inferior beauty." It is because of this distinction that many people mistake his words for an opposition against the unity of beauty, truth and goodness. Chapter 81 of *Laozi* reads,

> Truthful words may not be beautiful; beautiful words may not be truthful. A good man may not be eloquent; an eloquent man may not be

带来快感的东西，比如鲜艳华丽的色彩、悦耳动听的声音等等，是一些有形象、有色泽、有器物可感受的东西。但根据《老子》中俯拾皆是的辩证法思想："大成若缺"，"大盈若冲"，"大直若屈，大巧若拙，大辩若讷"（第四十五章），老子美学思想中那个至大至妙的形象——那个绝对"美"的标本，应该就是无形无名的、作为世界万物的总根源和最高本体的"道"。《老子》第四十一章说：

> 大方无隅，大器晚成，大音希声，大象无形，道隐无名。

大道周遍宇内而且通达万物，自然就十分隐微而不可知其形，不可称其名。"道"，即使人们把它描绘出来，也只是"淡兮其无味，视之不足见，听之不足闻，用之不足既"（第三十五章）。"既"是终结、穷尽的意思。从这个意义上讲，老子的"道"也就是后来庄子所谓"天地有大美而不言"❶中的"大美"。而平常人们所认为"美"的东西，如"五音"、"五色"、"美言"等等，在老子眼中都是"失道而后德，失德而后仁，失仁而后义，失义而后礼"的产物，都只是些庸人们津津乐道的"美"，即"小美"或"下美"。故老子对之一概加以否定，发出了"五色令人目盲，五音令人耳聋，五味令人口爽，驰骋畋猎令人心发狂，难得之货令人行妨"（第十二章）的尖锐批判。

也正是将"美"或美的艺术品（如"美言"、"辩"等），区别为"大美"、"上美"与"小美"、"下美"。所以老子又说出了许多被人误解为反对美与真、善统一的话来。《老子》第八十一章说：

> 信言不美，美言不信；善者不辩，辩者不善；知者不

---

❶《庄子·知北游》。

❶ "Zhibeiyou," *Zhuangzi*.

good. A wise man may not be learned; a learned man may not be wise.

In some people's eyes, Laozi attempted to reveal the contradiction among beauty, truth and goodness: Beauty is not truth, and truth is not beauty; goodness is not beauty, and beauty is not goodness. Some argue that we cannot simply affirm that Laozi was against the unity of beauty, truth and kindness. What we can conclude is that his views were formed from the standpoint of the critique against the civilized world, for at his time, there was frequent deviation of beauty from truth and goodness in society, sometimes even opposition of beauty to them.

Though these views all make sense, they are lopsided. Indeed, Laozi's words not only expose the contradiction among beauty, truth and goodness, but also criticize the phenomena in the realistic society, such as beauty without truth and goodness, and truth or goodness without beauty. However, we should be aware that Laozi's theory of beauty classifies beauty into "the most admirable beauty" and "the least admirable beauty," "the superior beauty" and " the inferior beauty." "The most admirable beauty" is "Tao." Chapter 21 reads,

Tao is opaque and obscure. Opaque and obscure, yet it has an image within; obscure and opaque, yet it has substance within. Dim and dark, yet it has a spirit within, which is genuine and filled with truth.

Although "Tao" is formless and nameless, it has an opaque and obscure image. So it is beautiful and can be used as the subject of aesthetics. Moreover, the mystical "most admirable beauty" also "has a spirit within," "filled with truth." In the ancient Chinese language, the character denoting "spirit" is interchangeable with "truth." It is obvious that "Tao" is genuine and trustworthy rather than fabricated. In other words, "Tao," or "the most admirable beauty," is a unification of truth, goodness and beauty, and there are no such phenomena in the realistic society as beauty without truth and goodness, truth and goodness without beauty. By saying "Truthful words may not be beautiful; beautiful words may not be truthful. A good man may not be eloquent; an eloquent man may not be good," Laozi pointed out the fact that in the realistic society, beauty, truth and goodness deviate from each other, inconsistent and contradictory. It only shows that the "beauty" Laozi mentioned here refers to "the least admirable beauty" and "the inferior beauty," which are totally different from "the most admirable beauty" mystically unified with "Tao."

博，博者不知。

有人说，老子这是在揭示美与真、善的矛盾和对立：美者不真，真者不美；善者不美，美者不善。有人说，不能简单断言老子反对美与真、善的统一，应该看到老子是立足于对文明社会批判的立场而发的，因为当时的社会存在着太多的美与真、善的背离，甚至是互相对立的事实。

这些看法都各有道理，但又都是失之偏颇的。老子的言论的确既揭露了美与真、善之间的矛盾对立，也批判了现实社会中美而不真、不善，或虽真虽善而不美的现象。但我们更应看到，老子论美实际是有"大美"与"小美"、"上美"与"下美"的区别的。"大美"就是"道"。《老子》第二十一章说：

> 道之为物，惟恍惟惚。惚兮恍兮，其中有象；恍兮惚兮，其中有物。窈兮冥兮，其中有精，其精甚真，其中有信。

"道"虽无形无名，但却有恍恍惚惚的形象。故而它是美的，可以作为人们审美的对象。而且这个玄妙的"大美"，还是"有精"、"有信"的。从古汉语来说，"其中有精"的"精"是个通假字，同"情"字，是"情实"的意思。可见，"道"是真实而不虚妄的，是真实而可信的。也就是说，"道"这个"大美"是真、善、美的统一，不存在美而不真、不善，或真、善而不美的现象。现在老子说"信言不美，美言不信；善者不辩，辩者不善。"指出现实生活中美与真、善互相背离、对立，而不相统一的事实，这只能说明老子此处所说的"美"是俗世间的"小美"、"下美"，而和与"道"玄同的"大美"是根本不同的。

2. Cleansing Your Mind's Eye (a Clean Mirror)

Laozi's aesthetic thought not only tells us what is beauty or what beauty is, but also let us know how to create and appreciate beauty.

Where Laozi surpasses his contemporary thinkers is, first of all, that he was the first person to clearly distinguish science from aesthetics in the history of Chinese aesthetics. Chapter 48 of *Laozi* says,

> He who pursues knowledge learns more day by day; he who pursues Tao does less day by day. Less and less is done until nothing is done at all; when nothing is done at all, nothing is left undone.

"Tao" is "the most admirable beauty," and vise versa, so "pursuing Tao" is the creation and appreciation of "the most admirable beauty," which is an aesthetic activity. According to Laozi, "He who pursues Tao does less day by day" is the basic principle and method of the aesthetic activity.

In Laozi's eyes, gaining specific knowledge and engaging in academic research are aimed at pursuing non-metaphysical specific knowledge, which is obtained through the perceptual experience. Through constantly accumulating the perceptual experience, people induce and analyze the numerous empirical materials, and then discard the dross and select the essential, eliminate the false and retain the true, make the analysis from this to that and from the surface to the centre, and continually obtain knowledge about the objective laws of things. Human knowledge has been accumulated from generation to generation, so it can be said, "He who pursues knowledge learns more day by day." "Learning more day by day" is directed against the method. But, the aesthetic activity is different, which requires comprehension and grasp of "Tao," that is, "the most admirable beauty." The "the most admirable beauty" is implied in "the sight of beauty is invisible; the sound of beauty is inaudible; the use of beauty is inexhaustible." In other words, "the most admirable beauty" is beyond the perceptual experience, so the inductive analysis of handling the empirical materials does not apply to attaining the knowledge of it. "Tao" ("the most admirable beauty") patterns itself after its own nature, quietly and with inaction, therefore, people must follow its example if they want to comprehend and grasp it. However, from childhood to adulthood, human beings have already accumulated lots of knowledge and prejudices, so it is quite hard for them to be natural and do nothing. The knowledge and prejudices can only be eliminated gradually. Just like "the fasting of the mind" said by Zhuangzi, you should first go on a fast for three, five and then seven

（二）涤除玄鉴

老子的美学思想不仅告诉了我们什么是美，或美是什么，同时还告诉我们应该如何进行审美创造和审美鉴赏。

老子超出了与他同时代的其他思想家的地方，首先在于他在中国美学史上第一次明确地区别了学术与审美的不同。《老子》第四十八章说：

> 为学日益，为道日损。损之又损，以至于无为，无为而无不为。

因为"道"就是"大美"，"大美"也就是"道"。所以，"为道"也就是对"大美"的创造与鉴赏，是一种审美活动。"为道日损"是老子提出的审美活动的基本原则和方法。

老子认为，学习具体知识和从事学术研究，其目的是追求形而下的具体知识，这种知识依靠感觉经验获得。人们通过不断积累感觉经验，对众多的经验材料进行归纳、分析，然后去粗取精，去伪存真，由此及彼，由表及里，不断获得对事物客观规律的认识。因为人类的知识是一代一代人日积月累、积少成多形成的，所以说"为学日益"。"日益"是一天天增加的意思，是就方法而言的。而审美活动则不同。审美活动要体悟、把握的是"道"，即是"大美"。这个"大美"是"视之不足见，听之不足闻，用之不足既"的，即是超越感觉经验的，所以不能用处理经验材料的那一套归纳分析的方法，来获得关于它的知识。因为"道"（"大美"）是效法自然的，是虚静无为的，因此，人类要体悟它、把握它，就必须效法它的样子，也要自然无为。但人类从童年到成年，已经积累了很多的知识和成见，要做到自然无为并不容易，只能逐渐地排除，像庄子讲的"心

days until you totally forget your own body, intelligence and knowledge and finally you can be natural and do nothing like "Tao" or "the most admirable beauty." Only when you attain what is implied in the statement that "a follower of Tao embraces Tao" (Chapter 23), can you obtain and comprehend "Tao" and "the most admirable beauty."

Laozi called this method "doing less." He said, "He who pursues Tao does less day by day. Less and less is done until nothing is done at all." Actually, people are required to reduce their desires, intrigues and deceits, prejudices and logical knowledge to the minimum when they are understanding Tao or "the most admirable beauty." At that point, people will correspond with the natural inaction of "Tao" or "the most admirable beauty," and can really obtain freedom and liberty. People are extricated from their prejudices, desires, intrigues and deceits, and logical knowledge so that they are totally free and naturally have "nothing left undone."

Of course, what Laozi said in "Less and less is done until nothing is done at all" is only a general principle and method of aesthetics, but "how to do less and less" is not easy to follow. As a result, Laozi further specified and clarified the principle and method, which is the so-called "cleansing your mind's eye." Chapter 10 says,

> Can you keep body and soul at one with Tao? Can you control your breath like a supple newly-born baby? Can you cleanse your mind's eye (a clean mirror) to rid it of all taint?

In fact, Laozi put forward a more specific aesthetic method, that is, we should not directly observe the aesthetic object; instead, we should start with the aesthetic subject and create a clean and transparent aesthetic mind.

Why "cleanse your mind's eye (a clean mirror)?" The reason is that it is closely related with "ridding it of all taint." *Explanatory Notes to Chinese Characters* interprets "taint" as "sickness." Then, how can the clean mirror get sick? It turns out to be a metaphor. Long time ago, the Chinese preferred to compare one's mind to a bright mirror, saying that the mind used to be as clear and clean as the mirror, shining and glorious. Later, no one knew when it was covered with dust and got dirty, that is to say, there was something wrong with it. Laozi referred to the dust as "taint." "Cleansing" is ridding the originally bright mind of the dust and making it clean again. According to Laozi, it is the

斋"那样，先斋戒三天、五天、七天，一直到把你的肢体、聪明、知识忘得干干净净，最后如"道"或"大美"那样，完全自然无为。"同于道者，道亦乐之得之。"（第二十三章）那时，你就可以获得或体悟到"道"与"大美"了。

老子把这种方法称之为"损"。"损"就是排除、减少的意思。老子说："为道日损，损之又损，以至于无为。"就是要人们在体悟、把握"道"或"大美"的时候，要把自己的私欲、智巧、成见和逻辑的知识，减少再减少，一天天地减少，减少到不能再减少的地步，这时候就与"道"或"大美"的自然无为相吻合了，人也就真正获得了自由和解放。人从自己的成见、私欲、智巧和逻辑知识中解放出来了，完全自由了，自然也就可以"无不为"了。

当然，老子说的"损之又损，以至于无为"，还只是一种审美的总的原则和方法，至于如何去"损之又损"，恐怕就不那么好操作了。所以，老子又进一步将这一原则方法具体化和明确化，这就是所谓"涤除玄鉴"。《老子》第十章说：

载营魄抱一，能无离乎？专气致柔，能婴儿乎？涤除玄览，能无疵乎？

老子这里实际上是提出了一个更具体明确的审美方法，即审美首先不是直接观照审美对象，而是先要从审美的主体开始，造就一个洁净透明的审美心胸。

为什么要"涤除玄鉴"呢？这是与下句"能无疵乎"密切相关的。《说文解字》对"疵"的解释是："病也。"那么，清澈明净的镜面怎么会生病呢？原来这是一个比喻。中国人很早就爱用明镜比喻人心，说人心本来和明镜一样清澈洁净，是很阳光的、很美好的，后来不知什么时候被染上了尘垢，弄脏了，也就是出毛病了。老子把这个染上的尘垢叫做"疵"。老子认

first thing for people to begin the creation of aesthetics. It is true not only of the cultivation of one's self, but also of the aesthetic activity in particular.

Then, what is the taint on the mirror? After all, only after finding it out can you rid yourself of it.

Throughout *Laozi*, there are internal taints and external ones in the grasp of "Tao" and the comprehension of "the most admirable beauty."

In terms of the external aspect, the taint refers to varieties of stimulating desires and greed caused by them. It can be seen from what Laozi said— the "five colors" that can blind the eye, the "five tones" that can deafen the ear, the "five tastes" that can dull the palate, "chasing and hunting" that can madden the mind, "rare goods" that can lure the heart. But, aren't the "five tones" and the "five colors" the beautiful works of art? Why did Laozi deny them? Because, according to Laozi, these things are only at most some "least admirable beauty" and "inferior beauty," rather than "Tao" or "the most admirable beauty" that he pursued. To regard them as "beautiful" or the "works of art" is only the common view, not Laozi's opinion. They cannot bring people the lofty spiritual transcendence or comfort; instead, they can only stimulate their desires and make them prisoners of lusts. Driven by the lusts, people will plunder crazily, totally putting aside "Tao" and "the most admirable beauty." Therefore, the first priority of the theory of Laozi's aesthetics is to rid people of the stimulating desires and greed caused by them. So, Chapter 3 reads,

> Not stimulating desires keeps people from confusion.

In terms of the internal aspect, Laozi thought that the taint deprives the mind of the real look of intrigues and deceits, hypocrisy and prejudices, including learning and knowledge that are gained through rational thinking. It is because of this that Laozi said, "Eliminate formalized wisdom and learning. Eliminate trickery and profiteering" (Chapter 19). However, in some people's eyes, Laozi did not object to people's probe into the objective world or the rational thinking method. For example, Chapter 54 reads, "Observe other people through your own self; observe other families through your own family; observe other villages through your own village; observe other countries through your own country." This is a typical analogical reasoning method, inferring the unknown from the known. We are of the opinion that Laozi was not generally opposed to the rational thinking and the results of its realization, but he, for the purpose of "pursuing Tao" or

为，这是人开始审美创造活动要做的第一件事。个人修身要这样，审美活动尤其要这样。

那么，被老子比喻为明镜上的瑕疵、尘垢的，都有哪些东西呢？

从《老子》全书来看，被老子看作妨碍人把握"道"或体悟"大美"的瑕疵，主要是内、外两方面的尘垢。

从外在方面来看，这种尘垢就是刺激人的欲望的各种外物及由此引起的人的贪欲。如老子所说的令人目盲的"五色"，令人耳聋的"五音"，令人口爽的"五味"，令人心发狂的"驰骋田猎"和使人行妨的"难得之货"。"五音"、"五色"不是美的艺术品吗？老子为什么连这些都要否定呢？因为在老子看来，这些东西充其量只是一些"小美"、"下美"，而不是他所要追求的"道"或"大美"。称其为"美"或艺术品，那只是世俗之见，并不是老子的观点。它们不仅不能给人带来高尚的精神超越和享受，反而会刺激人的欲望，使人变成欲望的俘虏，在欲望的驱使下疯狂地去攫取和掠夺，根本忘了"道"与"大美"。因此，老子的审美理论中第一要务，就是扫除刺激人的欲望的外物及由此引发的人的贪欲。《老子》第三章说：

> 不见可欲，使民心不乱。

从内在方面来看，老子认为这种尘垢就是使人心灵失去了本真状态的智巧、诈伪、成见，包括经过理性思维而形成的学问与知识。老子提出"绝圣弃智"、"绝巧弃利"（第十九章），也是这个原因。但有人却认为，老子并不反对人们去认识客观世界，并不反对理性思维的认识方法。例如，《老子》第五十四章中的"以身观身，以家观家，以乡观乡，以邦观邦，以天下观天下"，就是一种典型的由已知推出未知的类比推理方法。我们认为，老子的确并不一般地反对理性思维及其认识成果，

aesthetics, did take a clear-cut stand against "pursuing one's studies" and the rational thinking after distinguishing "pursuing one's studies" from "pursuing Tao." The best evidence is that Laozi repeatedly appealed, "Eliminate rote learning and you will have no worries" (Chapter 19 and 20). Chapter 56 reads,

> Curb your senses and guard the door to your heart; conceal your brilliance and be as humble as dust; blunt your sharpness and untangle your knots. This is known as "mystical union with virtue."

In terms of the inner mind, such a person can be as simple as a newborn baby, as ignorant as a "fool." Thus, he can indeed grasp "Tao" and comprehend "the most admirable beauty." But, in terms of the methodology, Laozi just talked about how to "cleanse your mind's eye to rid it of all taint."

3. "Flavors without Attending Grand Feasts" and "Wonderful Images"

Besides telling us what is beauty and the principles and methods concerning aesthetics, Laozi's aesthetic thought establishes some important aesthetic concepts, such as "nonbeing," "wonder," "taste" and "image," and it also depicts an ideal aesthetic realm.

Whether a system of aesthetic thought is established depends on whether it has formed its own set of concepts and a system of terms, which is a very important symbol. Chinese aesthetics has a system with its unique concepts and categories, so it is undoubtedly a mature form of aesthetics.

Laozi is the real founder of Chinese aesthetics. It should be said that he indeed established some important concepts and categories in Chinese aesthetics, such as "being," "nonbeing," "fiction," "truth," "beauty," "evil" (ugliness), "wonder," "taste," "breath" and "image," and in particular, the concepts of "nonbeing," "wonder," "taste" and "image" have exerted great influence on Chinese aesthetics for thousands of years.

Prior to Laozi, concepts of "nonbeing," "fiction," "evil," "taste," and "image" were used in Chinese academic thinking, but most of them were only used in terms of the common sense. For example, "nonbeing" only indicated that some external thing or existence did not exist in some specific time and

但老子的确是在区分了"为学"与"为道"之后，在"为道"的目标下旗帜鲜明地反对"为学"和理性思维的。老子反复呼吁"绝学无忧"（第十九章、第二十章），就是最好的证明。《老子》第五十六章说：

> 塞其兑，闭其门，挫其锐，解其纷，和其光，同其尘，是谓玄同。

从内心的境界来说，能这样做的人，就能和初生的婴儿一样单纯，像"愚人"一样无知，也就能真正地把握"道"、体悟"大美"。而如果从方法论上看，老子也就是在说如何"涤除玄鉴"。

（三）"无味"与"妙象"

老子的美学思想，除了告诉我们什么是美和有关审美的原则方法之外，还创立了一些重要美学概念，如"无"、"妙"、"味"、"象"等等，并为我们描绘出了一种理想的审美境界。

一种美学思想体系是否已经建立，其中一个重要标志就是看它是否已经形成了自己的一套概念和术语系统。中国美学是有自己独特的概念、范畴体系的，因此它无疑已是一种成熟的美学形态。

老子是中国美学的真正开山者。中国美学中的一些概念、范畴，如"有"、"无"、"虚"、"实"、"美"、"恶"（丑）、"妙"、"味"、"气"、"象"等，应该说都是由老子真正确立的，特别是"无"、"妙"、"味"、"象"等概念，对此后中国数千年的美学产生了重大的影响。

在老子之前，中国的学术思想中也使用"无"、"虚"、"恶"、"味"、"象"等概念，但大多只是在常识的层面上加以使用。如："无"，只是表明某个外物或存在物不存在于某一具体的时

space. "Fiction" indicated that there was no physical evidence to prove the existence of things. "Taste" meant the feeling that people had in their mouths when eating something. The Chinese character "image" originally referred to "elephant," but later it referred to the specific image. Anyway, all these concepts were only used according to the experience in daily life or the common sense, and they had little to do with aesthetics.

The concept of "nonbeing" in Laozi's aesthetic thought and "being" are always integrated, opposite and complementary to each other. In the statements "Being and nonbeing are two phases of existence" (Chapter 2) and "therefore, benefit comes from being; usefulness comes from nonbeing" (Chapter 11), the word "nonbeing" already has the well-defined meaning of philosophical dialectics. Laozi further extended the "nonbeing" to aesthetics and associated it with "shape," "image" and "taste." Thus, "nonbeing" not only had the profound meaning in aesthetics, in the later history of Chinese aesthetics, but also evolved into the development of aesthetics, in which "being" is sought from "nonbeing." "Silence is better than sound" in music appreciation and "blank-leaving" in the graphic arts in China are actually the application and evolution of the concept of "nonbeing" in Laozi's aesthetic thought.

Similarly, "taste" is also the concept first introduced into the field of aesthetics by Laozi. He said, "Tao speaks for itself, 'The taste of me is insipid' " (Chapter 35) and "Act without taking visible actions; work without making major exertion; savor flavors without attending grand feasts" (Chapter 33). "Savor" here does not refer to the taste, but the feeling when one listens to others. It is an aesthetic comprehension. The Chinese refer to the comprehension of "Tao" and "the most admirable beauty" as "appreciating images" and "appreciating Tao." For example, "appreciating images with a pure mind" and "appreciating Tao with a pure mind" put forward in the Southern and Northern dynasties regarded "insipid taste" as one of the highest aesthetic criteria and a kind of aesthetic style was thus established, which was called "insipidness." All these are unique in the world.

"Wonder" is also an aesthetic category, first established by Laozi. "Wonder" means "goodness" ❶ in early Chinese dictionaries. In other words, it means that a woman is beautiful. However, Laozi referred to it specifically as the wonder of "Tao" and "the most admirable beauty." He said, "Be always

空之中，这就是"无"；"虚"，也只是表示事物没有实物可以验证；"味"，则是人吃东西时在口里的感觉；"象"，本是指"象"这种动物，后来发展到表示各种具体的物象。但这些都只是根据日常生活的经验或常识而使用的概念，与美学关系不大。

老子美学思想中的"无"概念，是始终和"有"相反相成、互相统一在一起的。"有无相生"（第二章）；"有之以为利，无之以为用"（第十一章）。这个"无"，已有鲜明的哲学辩证法的意义。老子又进一步将这个"无"引入到美学，将它和"状"、"象"、"味"联系起来，不仅使它具有了浓厚的美学意义，而且还使它在后来的中国美学史上发展形成了一条在"无"中求"有"的美学路向。中国人音乐鉴赏中的所谓"无声胜有声"，书画艺术中的"留白"等等，实际都是老子美学思想中"无"概念的运用和衍生。

同样，"味"也是老子将它首先引入到美学领域的。老子说："道之出口，淡乎无味。"（第三十五章）"为无为，事无事，味无味"。（第三十三章）这个"味"不是吃东西的味道，而是体味、品味的"味"，是一种审美的体悟。中国人把对"道"、对"大美"的体悟称作"味象"、"味道"——如南北朝时提出"澄怀味象"、"澄怀味道"，把"淡乎无味"当作最高的审美标准之一，形成了一种称为"平淡"的审美风格。这些在世界上是独一无二的。

"妙"，也是老子首先建立起来的美学范畴。"妙"字，中国早期词典的解释是："好也"❶，即指女子长得美丽。但老子则用以专指"道"、"大美"形象的微妙。老子说："故常有欲，

---

❶《广雅·释诂一》。

❶ "Shigu," *Guangya*.

passionate to detect its wonders. From mystery to mystery leads this gateway to all wonders" (Chapter 1). Wang Bi said, "Wonder is the most subtle." ❶ Therefore, Laozi also said, "The ancient sages who were followers of Tao were miraculously perceptive and unfathomly profound." "Wonder" can be said to be a kind of "being," but it is a profound "being." The aesthetic category "wonder" remolded by Laozi does not refer to the beauty of women, nor does it refer to the beauty in general; instead, it refers in particular to a meaningful form. Thereafter, in the field of Chinese aesthetics, beauty with implications, beauty well worth the appreciation and beauty giving much food for thought have been described with "wonder," such as "wonderful writing," "wonderful statements," "wonderful essays," "wonderful dances," "wonderful colors," "wonderful appearances," "wonderful tones," "wonderful persons" and "wonderful looks."

"Image" was also first introduced by Laozi into the field of aesthetics. Laozi said, "Tao is opaque and obscure. Opaque and obscure, yet it has an image within; obscure and opaque, yet it has substance within" (Chapter 11). This "image" is opaque and obscure and, though formless, can be touched and "grasped" (Chapter 35 and 41). It has already depicted "Tao" as the work of art of "beauty." Most important of all, the "image" in Laozi's aesthetic thought is neither a specific image, nor a ready-made work of art; instead, it is the product of the people's aesthetic imagination and recreation. "Explaining Laozi" of *Han Feizi* says, "The live elephant is seldom seen, so people imagine how the live elephant looks according to the dead ones' skeletons. As a result, people refer to what they imagine getting as 'elephant' " (homophone with image in Chinese). It is shown that Laozi's "image" has already become an aesthetic category, an imagined product which is processed by art. Since then, in Chinese aesthetics, the concepts of "appreciating images," "absorbing images" and "breathing images" have been further developed from the concept of "image" in Laozi's aesthetics.

Of course, like the entire traditional Chinese theories of philosophy and aesthetics, all of Laozi's aesthetic concepts, categories, propositions and the establishment of the system of his aesthetic thought are not aimed at constructing a completely theoretical system, but establishing a perfect personality ideal and attaining a spiritual realm of realizing oneness with "Tao" and "oneness of nature and man." According to him, this is the biggest joy of

以观其妙。""玄之又玄，众妙之门。"（第一章）王弼解释"妙"字说："妙者，微之极也。"❶ 所以，老子又说："古之善为道者，微妙玄通，深不可识。""妙"可以说是一种"有"，但是一种很深微的"有"。经老子改造过后的美学范畴"妙"，不再仅指女人的美，甚至也不指一般意义上的美，而是特指一种有意味的形式。此后，中国美学领域凡有意蕴、值得人反复品鉴、回味的美，就被用"妙"字来形容，如"妙笔"、"妙句"、"妙篇"、"妙舞"、"妙色"、"妙相"、"妙音"、"妙人"、"妙容"等等。

"象"，也是老子首先引入美学领域的概念。老子说："道之为物，惟恍惟惚。惚兮恍兮，其中有象；恍兮惚兮，其中有物。"（第十一章）这个"象"，"惟恍惟惚"、缥缈朦胧，虽"无形"却可以感触，可以"执"（第三十五章、第四十一章）。这就已经把"道"描绘成了"美"的艺术品。更重要的是，老子美学思想中的这个"象"，它并不是具体的形象，也不是现成的艺术品，而是人们审美想象或再创造的产物。《韩非子·解老篇》说："人很少见到活象，而得一具死象的骨骼，依据死象的骨骼想见活象的样子，所以人们把据臆想得到的东西都叫象。"这说明，老子的"象"已是一个美学范畴，是艺术加工、想象的产物。此后中国美学中的"味象"、"取象"、"意象"、"气象"等概念，也都是由老子美学中的"象"概念进一步发展而来的。

当然，与整个中国传统的哲学、美学理论一样，老子所有美学概念、范畴、命题的提出，老子整个美学思想体系的建立，并不是为了建构一个完整t的理论系统，而是为了建立起一种完美的人格理想，为了实现与"道"合一或"天人合一"的精神境界。老子认为，那才是人生的最大的快乐和审美的最终目的。

❶ 王弼：《老子注》第一章。

❶ Chapter 1 of *Commentaries on Laozi* by Wang Bi.

one's life and the ultimate goal of aesthetics. Thus, he said, "Therefore, a follower of Tao embraces Tao; a follower of virtue embraces virtue" (Chapter 23). Such a person will be the happiest in the world.

老子说："故从事于道的人，就能与道合同为一，从事于德的人，就能与德合同为一"；"与道合同为一的人，道也就很乐于得到他；与德合同为一的人，德也就很乐于得到他。"（第二十三章）这样的人，是世界上最快乐的人。

福建清源山老子雕像

The Sculpture of Laozi in Qingyuan Mountain of Fujian Province

八 老子思想在中国思想史上的地位和影响

Chapter Ⅷ   The Position and Influence of Laozi's Thought in the History of Chinese Thought

With unique and profound wisdom in regard to the root and generation of all things, social politics, life and the theory of aesthetics, Laozi's thought has made a great contribution to the formation of the way of thinking in the traditional Chinese philosophy. It has a very important position and influence.

First of all, the position and influence of his thought in the history of Chinese thought are embodied by the fact that he initiated the theory concerning the origin and root of all things in Chinese philosophy, that is, ontology in philosophy. The ideological history is multi-level, including politics, economy, social ethics, educational psychology, arts and esthetics, philosophy and academic science. Among so many fields, philosophy is the study of making the overall exploration of the universe and life, playing a guiding role in the other ideological fields.

On the whole, the Confucian School and the Taoist School have undoubtedly made the greatest contribution and exerted the strongest influence on the Chinese culture. In general, the Chinese culture has a dual structure, in which Confucianism and Taoism are mutually exclusive and complementary with each other. It is also true of the philosophical thought.

The philosophical thought of Confucianism is an important part of the Chinese philosophy. It has exerted more influence than Taoism on the secular society of China, especially the ancient official thought. After the Confucian School was established by Confucius, its theory was focused on the social ethics, and an entire set of moral norms and norms of propriety between the sovereign and the ministers, between the father and the son, and between the brothers were set up, such as humaneness, righteousness, propriety, wisdom and fidelity. However, it showed little interest in and tended to ignore the origin of all things and the basis for their existence. Confucius seldom mentioned "Tao" or "the Tao of heaven," which was the first principle and the general law of the world. As Confucius' disciple, Zigong said, "The Master's discourses about man's nature, and the way of Heaven, cannot be heard." ❶ In other words, Confucius seldom mentioned the issue of humanity and root of all beings.

Ontology in the Chinese philosophy was initiated by the Taoist School, or specifically, by Laozi. In Chinese philosophical history, Laozi was the first person to clarify the metaphysical feature of "Tao" and the feature of its existence before all things. This can be seen in what he said, "A formless entity

老子思想在关于天地万物的总根源及其生成，关于社会政治、人生以及审美理论等方面，都有着独特而深刻的智慧，为中华民族传统思想和文化的形成，做出了突出的贡献，具有重要的地位和影响。

老子思想在中国思想史上的地位和影响，首先是他开创了中国哲学关于天地万物的起源和本根的理论，即哲学的本体论。思想史有很多的层面，包括政治的、经济的、社会伦理的，教育心理的、艺术和审美的，也包括哲学和学术的等等。而在这诸多的领域中，哲学是对宇宙人生进行整体性探索的学科，对其他思想领域起着指导作用。

就总体而言，对中国古代文化贡献和影响最大的，无疑是儒家和道家。中国文化总体上是一个由儒道互斥到互补的二元结构，在哲学思想方面也是如此。

儒家哲学思想是中国哲学的重要组成部分。它对中国世俗社会，特别是古代官方意识形态的影响可能还在道家之上。但儒家自孔子开始以来，就把他们的理论重心放在社会伦理方面，建立起了君臣、父子、兄弟之间的一整套道德规范和礼仪制度，如：仁、义、礼、智、信（圣）等。而对于关于天地万物的起源和存在根据的问题，儒家则兴趣不大，往往多有忽略。孔子就罕言作为世界本原和总规律的"道"或"天道"，孔子的学生子贡说："夫子之言性与天道，不可得而闻也。"❶ 即听不到孔子谈人性与万物的根源问题。

中国哲学的本体论是由道家开创的，具体地说，即是由老子开创的。老子在中国哲学史上首次明确阐明了"道"的形上性质和它先在于万物的性质。他说："有物混成，先天地生。

❶《论语·公冶长》。
❶ "Gongye Chang," *Lunyu*.

existed prior to heaven and earth. Silent and void, it stands alone and unchanging, the mother of all things under heaven. Not knowing its name, I call it 'Tao' " (Chapter 25). "Tao" is formless and nameless, so Laozi also said, "The nameless Tao is the origin of all things" (Chapter 1); "All things are born from some being, which is born from the nonbeing of Tao" (Chapter 40). In the history of Chinese philosophical thought, the theories of his "Tao" first clearly referred to "Tao" as the origin and root of all things, that is to say, the entity of all things. It symbolized the formal birth of ontology in the Chinese philosophy.

After Laozi, metaphysicians of the Wei and Jin dynasties also paid much attention to the first principle and entity of the world, saying that "all things are nothingness-oriented;" while the Neo-Confucians of the Song Dynasty were of the opinion that "principle" (*li* in Chinese) was the foundation for the existence of the world. Though different from Laozi's viewpoint, Neo-Confucianism was obviously influenced by Laozi and followed his thought. Therefore, according to some contemporary historians of philosophy in China, the ontology of Laozi and Zhuangzi was the source of theory of the ontological thought of later ages. While we hold that without Laozi's ontological thought, the Chinese philosophy would have invited ridicule from Westerners, it would still have contained some doctrines of ethics only, and it would have not developed the philosophical thought.

The position and influence of Laozi's thought in the history of Chinese thought are also embodied as follows. As Taoist alchemists in ancient China repeatedly quoted and sought connections with him, Laozi was finally venerated as the highest god in the pedigree of Taoist immortals while his thought was organized into the Taoist doctrines.

Taoism is the native religion of China, immortal worship being its feature, attaining immortality being its highest goal. The birth of Taoism is related to nature worship, god and ghost worship, and necromancy in ancient times while its direct source is the immortal alchemy during the Warring States Period and the Qin and Han dynasties. However, Taoism as a religion was originally different from that as a school of thought, and Laozi and his thought had nothing to do with the immortal alchemy at the very beginning.

寂兮寥兮，独立而不改，周行而不殆，可以为天下母。吾不知其名，强字之曰道。"（第二十五章）一个先于天地万物产生的"混成"之物，寂寥虚静，无物可比，运化万物，永不停息，是天地万物的本源。这个独立永恒之物，作者无法给它命名，勉强给它取名字叫"道"。"道"无形无名，所以老子又说："无名，天地之始。"（第一章）"天下万物生于有，有生于无"。（第四十章）老子的这些"道"论，在中国哲学思想史上，第一次明确地把"道"作为天地万物的总根源和总根据，也就是以"道"作为天地万物的本体。这标志着中国哲学本体论的正式诞生。

在老子之后，魏晋时期的玄学家们也十分关注世界的本源和本体，提出了"天地万物以无为本"；宋代理学家则认为，"理"是世界存在的根据。虽然与老子的观点不同，却明显受到了老子观点的影响，是沿着老子的思路发展的。所以，有的中国现代哲学史家说，"老（庄）子的本体论是后代无本论思想的理论源泉。"我们则说：如果没有老子确立的本体论思想，中国哲学也许确实会成为西方人所嘲笑的那样，只有一些伦理学说，还没有发展出哲学的思辨。

老子思想在中国思想史上的地位和影响还表现为，在中国古代道教方术之士的不断援用和攀附之下，老子最终被附会成了道教神仙谱系中的最高神，而老子的思想也被组织进了道教的教义。

道教是中国的本土宗教，神仙崇拜是它的特征，得道成仙是它的最高目标。道教的产生与远古时代的自然崇拜、鬼神崇拜和巫术有关，战国秦汉时代的神仙方术是它的直接来源。但是，道教作为宗教，与道家作为思想流派原本不同；老子及其思想最初与神仙方术更没有关系。

In the Warring States Period, all vassal states were carrying out politic reforms, attempting to become stronger when the "Studies of Huang and Lao" quietly flourished. Based on the words of Huang Di (the Yellow Emperor) in ancient times, the Studies incorporated Laozi's Tao, discoursed on Legalism in terms of Tao and absorbed the advantages of various schools. The "Studies of Huang and Lao," on the one hand, advocated the political reforms and government by law; on the other hand, it took Laozi's thought, such as complying with the Tao of heaven and humanity, nature worship and objection to artificial intervention, as the basis for the reforms to prove the rationality and feasibility of the government by law. The "Huang and Lao" scholars gave lectures mainly in Jixia in the state of Qi, so they were called the "School of Huang and Lao in Jixia." This was the first connection of Laozi's thought with the Taoist doctrines.

In the early Western Han Dynasty, the society badly needed to rest and build up strength. Both the emperors and the empress dowagers were fond of the "Studies of Huang and Lao," and thus, Laozi's thought of "being quiet and doing nothing" once became the tactics of administering the country of the time. Scholars also elucidated, summarized and developed his thought by annotating *Laozi* or compiling works. Representative in this area are *Laozi's Intention* by Yan Junping, *Commentaries on Laozi* by Heshanggong and *Huainanzi* by King Huainan, Liu An. At the end of the Eastern Han Dynasty, the Studies of Huang and Lao was further connected with the immortal alchemy in the society, thus, Taoism was finally established. If it might be said that "Taiping Taoism" as the political organization was utterly suppressed, "Wudoumi Taoism" ("Five Pecks of Rice Taoism" or Tianshi Taoism) founded by Zhang Daoling in the Bashu region could be regarded as the symbol of the formal establishment of Taoism. Besides some religious discipline ceremonies, such as providing five pecks of rice and first-class prayer, Wudoumi Taoism's biggest connection with Laozi's thought was "offering libation with *Laozi* containing 5 000 Chinese characters." Everyone must learn *Laozi* at the time. Laozi was deified by the almost contemporaneous Taoism *Scripture of Great Peace* and the *Xiang'er Commentaries on Laozi*. The two books called him "the Emperor of Nine Mysteries" and the "Most Exalted Lord Lao" respectively.

During the Wei, Jin, Southern and Northern dynasties, *Internal Piece* of *Baopuzi* by Ge Hong of the Jin Dynasty called Laozi's Tao "*xuan yi*," "*yuan yi*" and "*zhen yi*," testifying the theory of Taoism immortality; while Lu Xiujing and Tao Hongjing of the Southern and Northern dynasties listed and

战国时候，各诸侯国都在变法图强。一种依托远古黄帝立言，并拉扯上老子，形成道法结合、以道论法、兼采百家的"黄老之学"悄悄地兴盛起来。"黄老之学"一方面依托黄帝，主张变法，实行法治；另一方面又把老子思想中顺应天道人性、崇尚自然、反对人为干预的思想内容，作为他们变法的根据，论证他们实行法治的合理性和可行性。这些黄老学者主要聚集于齐国的稷下讲学，因此就有人把他们称为"稷下黄老学派"。这是老子思想与道教教义发生关联的第一步。

西汉初期，社会急需休养生息。汉初的皇帝、太后都好"黄老之学"，老子清净无为的思想一度成为当时的治国之术。文人们也通过注释《老子》或个人著述，阐释、总结和发展老子的思想。严君平的《老子指归》、河上公的《老子注》、淮南王刘安的《淮南子》等，都是这方面的代表作。东汉末年，黄老之学与社会上的神仙方术进一步结合，道教最终得以创立。如果说"太平道"作为一种政治组织而被彻底镇压下去了的话，那么张道陵在巴蜀地区创建的"五斗米道"（或称"天师道"），则可以看成是道教正式成立的标志。"五斗米道"除了有出五斗米、祈祷首过等宗教戒规仪式之外，与老子思想的最大关联，是"祭酒主以《老子》五千文"，大家都得学习《老子》。而差不多同时的道教《太平经》和《老子想尔注》，则把老子加以神化，分别称为"九玄帝君"和"太上老君"。

魏晋南北朝时，先有葛洪的《抱朴子·内篇》，把老子的道称为"玄一"、"元一"、"真一"，以论证道教长生成仙的理

expounded on the pedigree of immortals, honoring Laozi as "the Universally Honored One of Tao and Virtues."

The Tang Dynasty claimed itself to be "the descendent of Laozi." Emperor Gaozong ordained Laozi "the Supreme Emperor of the Mysterious Origin," ordering the officials to study and learn *Laozi* and adding it to the imperial civil examination. Emperor Taizong ordained Laozi as "the Ancestor of the Great Saint with Tao and the Supreme Emperor of the Mysterious Origin of the Golden Imperial Palace" and personally annotated *Tao Te Ching*, thus, Laozi's thought had even higher status in Taoism.

The Song and Yuan dynasties witnessed the division of Taoism into the northern and southern schools. Further integrated with Confucianism and Buddhism, Laozi's thought incorporated the Taoism theory of health preservation into the cultivation of spiritual nature and bodily life, as well as the theory of mind-nature.

There are many ambiguities about Laozi's life, such as the different legends about him, Lao Dan, Lao Laizi and the historiographer Dan, and different versions about his life span, which are recorded in "The Biography of Laozi and Han fei" of the *Records of the Grand Historian*. Throughout *Laozi*, there are also many mysterious accounts about Tao, and the opinions about how to "excel in preserving one's life" or preserve one's health, such as "this is called 'deep-rootedness,' the way of long life and eternal vision" and "those who excel in preserving their lives never meet tigers in the hills." All these make it possible for Taoism to establish its doctrines by quoting and interpreting Laozi's thought.

The theory of "Tao," the theory of "virtue" and the thought of health preservation were mainly interpreted and quoted by Taoism. Laozi said, "Tao gives birth to and virtue nurtures all things" (Chapter 51); "From Tao comes oneness; from oneness comes the duality of *yin* and *yang*; from duality comes the equilibrium of *yin* and *yang*; from equilibrium comes all things under heaven." Taoism, on the other hand, further personalized and deified "Tao," which was finally combined with Laozi into oneness. The combination thus became the Most Honored God which produced all things. the *Xiang' er Commentaries on Laozi*, an early Taoism scripture says, "'Oneness' is 'Tao' .... When 'oneness' is separated, it will become *qi* (breath), which is congregated into the 'Most Exalted Lord Lao.'" Wang Fu of the Eastern Han Dynasty even directly identified Laozi with "Tao" in his *Tablet of the Venerable Master's Saintly Mother*. From then on, the Taoist classics had been making up legends about Laozi's creating the world, with one being refined than another.

论；后有南北朝时的陆修静、陶弘景等人列叙神仙谱系，把老子尊为"道德天尊"。

李唐王朝自称"老君子孙"，唐高宗追封老子为"太上玄元皇帝"，命百官研习《老子》，科举加试《老子》；唐太宗又加尊老子为"大圣祖高上大道金阙玄元天皇大帝"，亲注《道德经》，使老子思想在道教中具有了更崇高的地位。

宋元时期，道教出现了南北分立的局面，老子思想和儒、佛进一步融合，由提倡性命双修、明心见性而融入道教内丹之学。

老子的生平中本有许多模糊之处，《史记·老子韩非列传》就记载有老子与老聃、老莱子、太史儋的不同传说，以及关于老子的年寿的不同说法。《老子》一书中也有许多对于道的神秘描述，还有关于如何"摄生"或养生的观点，如"深根固柢，长生久视之道"；"善摄生者，陆行不遇兕虎，入军不被甲兵"等。这些都为道教援附老子思想以建立其教义，提供了某种思想资源。

被道教附会、援用的老子思想，主要是其中的"道"论、"德"论以及养生思想。老子说："道生之，德畜之"（第五十一章）；"道生一，一生二，二生三，三生万物"（第四十二章）。道教则进一步将"道"人格化和神格化，最后"道"与老子合二为一，成为创生万物的至尊神。早期的道教秘籍《老子想尔注》就说："'一'就是'道'……'一'离散就形成为气，聚集就形成为'太上老君'。"东汉王阜的《圣母碑》更直接说老子就是"道"。从此以后的道教经典，便不断地编造出一个比一个精致的老子创生世界的神话。

In addition, Taoism also associated Laozi's thought about "virtue" with the religious ethics. Laozi advocated "superior virtue," "mystical virtue" and "mighty virtue." He said, "Giving birth without possessing, working without taking credit and guiding without dominating: This is called 'mystical virtue' " (Chapter 51). He advocated the natural virtue of doing nothing while Taoism imposed an inaccurate interpretation on Laozi's "virtue" and extended it into the religious ethics and the Confucian concepts. "Dui Su" of *Internal Piece* of *Baopuzi* by Ge Hong said, "He who seeks immortality must put first loyalty and filial piety, amiability and obedience, humaneness and faithfulness. If he only pursues alchemy without cultivating his own virtues, he will not attain longevity." Therefore, later on, the *Scripture of the Void Nature of the Most Exalted Lord Lao* also said, "A man of virtue excels in attaining good deeds and merits." Thus, Laozi's thought of "virtue" became the moral principles and ethics of loyalty and filial piety, humaneness and righteousness, assuming the social function of encouraging the good and punishing the evil.

According to Laozi, all things under heaven came from the equilibrium of *yin* and *yang*. He elucidated how to preserve health. Taoism extended these thoughts into the pursuit of alchemy of immortality. Laozi said, "Heaven and earth enjoy longevity—their selflessness gives them longevity" (Chapter 7); "Cultivate virtue in yourself, and virtue will be genuine" (Chapter 54); and "All things embody *yin* and *yang* as opposing parts; the blending of both brings equilibrium" (Chapter 42). However, Taoism interpreted "longevity" as immortality and extended "keeping body and soul at one with Tao" and "the blending of both" into "immortality by attaining mental tranquility" and the method of practicing *yin* and *yang*. In other words, the body was reckoned as the oven, the vitality *yin* and *yang* as the medicine and "soul" as the fire, and then pills of immortality could be made.

The position and influence of Laozi's thought are also embodied as follows: It is a very important medium and link in the integration of Confucianism, Buddhism and Taoism in the history of Chinese thought. From the Warring States Period to the Qin and Han dynasties, the "Studies of Huang and Lao" advocated the absorption of the advantages of Confucianism and Mohism and the distillation of the School of Logicians and Legalism. Though this opinion was based on the "words of Huang Di," it was mainly from Laozi's thought. No matter scholars in Jixia or the "Huang and Lao" scholars, they could find resources of thought from Laozi's viewpoint that "the sage governs by doing nothing and governs a large country as if cooking a small

此外，道教还把老子关于"德"的思想往宗教伦理方面做了发挥。老子崇尚的是"上德"、"玄德"、"大德"。老子说："生产万物而不占有，化成万物却不自恃有功，为万物之长却不宰制它们，这就叫作玄德。"（第五十一章）他倡导的是自然无为的品德，但道教却将老子的"德"往宗教伦理和儒家道德观上加以附会、引申。葛洪的《抱朴子·内篇·对俗》说："欲求仙者，要当以忠孝、和顺、仁信为本，若德行不修，而但务求方术，皆不得长生也。"故后来的《老君太上虚无自然本起经》又说："德者，谓为善之功德也。"老子的"德"思想就变成了忠孝仁义的纲常伦理，承担起了劝善禁恶的社会功能。

道教又把老子的万物由阴阳二气和合而成的思想及人如何修身养生的思想，引申、附会为追求长生不死和得道成仙的仙术。老子说："天地之所以能长且久者，以其不自生，故能长生。"（第七章）"修之身，其德乃真。"（第五十四章）"万物负阴而抱阳，冲气以为和。"（第四十二章）道教却将老子的"长生久视"，附会为长生不死，将老子的"抱一"、"冲气"之说，引申为"养神不死"和炼气之法。即所谓以己身为炉，以体内的精气为药物，以"神"为炉火，进行烧炼的"内丹术"。

老子思想在中国思想史上的地位和影响，第三个方面的表现，就是它在中国思想史上的儒、释、道的融合中，发挥了重要的中介和纽带作用。自战国至秦汉时期，黄老之学"采儒、墨之善，撮名、法之要"，其中所依托的除了"黄帝之言"外，很重要的就是老子的思想。老子思想中的圣人无为而治、"治大国若烹小鲜"的主张，无论是稷下学者，还是汉初的黄老学

fish." In the Wei and Jin dynasties, the integration of Confucianism and Taoism was also realized through the medium—Laozi's thought. For example, according to Laozi, "All things are born from some being, which is born from the nonbeing of Tao," but He Yan and Wang Bi interpreted it as "all things are nothingness-oriented" and established the "Doctrine of Nothingness." However, in Wang Bi's opinion, Laozi overemphasized "nonbeing," so he actually advocated "being" and was no match for Confucius who was a silent "sage." Starting in view of Laozi's thought, Wang Bi reconciled Confucianism and Taoism by criticizing and sublating the weaknesses in the thought. When Buddhism was introduced into China, it also started from the far-fetched comparison with Laozi's thought. A famous case in point is that "Six Schools and Seven Sects" in the Eastern and Western Jin dynasties publicized "nothingness" to appreciate and elucidate "emptiness" in Buddhism. In the Tang Dynasty, Buddhism was further localized, and the appearance of the Zen sect was one of its symbols. The Zen sect was divided into the Northern sect and the Southern sect. In the practice of Buddhism, the Northern sect emphasized "gradual practice" while the Southern sect "epiphany." Master Shenxiu of the Northern sect had a gatha which reads, "Body is like a bodhi tree, while mind is like a bright mirror. Do frequently clean it so as to get rid of dust." As we know, Laozi had a statement that "cleansing your mind's eye to rid it of all taint." It also compared one's mind to a bright mirror, which must be kept clean by ridding all taint. Thus, it can be said that "cleansing your mind's eye to rid it of all taint" was reflected in Shenxiu's practice of Buddhism. It can also be said that Laozi's thought played a bridging and linking role in the process of Buddhism being localized in China.

Finally, the position and influence of Laozi's thought are also reflected in the fact that the thought laid some foundations and the development for ancient Chinese aesthetics. For example, Laozi said, "A thunderous sound seems mute; an immense image seems shapeless;" "Being and nonbeing are two phases of existence." This laid the foundation for some theories in ancient Chinese aesthetics, such as "pursuing excellence," "writing truth with fiction" and "mutual promotion between truth and fiction." Therefore, ancient Chinese aesthetics emphasized that articles should have the "implied meanings," poems should "use the form to show the spirit" and "stand in the centre of the ring" (of thought), music should pursue overtones and linger in the air, and paintings should contain truth and fiction, with the mutual promotion between them, being like cloud and fog, without giving out delicate fragrance, being wonderful beyond words, and being invisible and unpredictable. In this way, it

者，都能从中找到所需要的思想资源。魏晋时期，儒、道的融合，也是以老子思想为中介实现的。何晏、王弼把老子的"天下万物生于有，有生于无"，解释为"天地万物以无为本"，建立起了"无本论"。但是王弼又认为，老子过于强调"无"，已落入第二义，实际上是个"有者"，赶不上孔子是一个沉默的"圣人"。这是从老子思想出发，通过批判和扬弃老子思想的弱点来调和儒道。佛教进入中国后，也是从比附老子思想开始的。两晋之间的"六家七宗"，大讲"本无"、"本无异"，用以理解和阐释佛教的般若"空"义，就是很著名的例子。唐代佛教进一步中国化，禅宗的出现是其标志之一。禅宗分为北宗和南宗。从修持方法上看，北宗强调"渐修"，南宗强调"顿悟"。北宗神秀大师有偈说："身如菩提树，心如明镜台，时时勤拂拭，莫使惹尘埃。"我们知道，老子修身有"涤除玄鉴"之说，也是把心比喻为明镜，要扫除上面的尘垢，使它恢复清澈。可以说，神秀的修持方法中有老子"涤除玄鉴"的影子。也可以说，老子思想在佛教中国化的过程中，起到了某种桥梁和纽带的作用。

最后，老子思想在中国思想史上的地位和影响，还表现为老子思想奠定了中国古代美学思想的某些基础和发展方向。例如，老子说："大音希声，大象无形"；"有无相生"。这就奠定了中国古代美学思想追求超越，以虚写实、虚实相生的理论基础。所以，中国古代美学强调文章要有"文外之旨"，诗歌要"超以象外，得其环中"，音乐要追求弦外之音、余音绕梁，绘画要有实有虚、虚实相生，如云如雾，幽香不吐，

was thought to attain the effect with endless interest and charm. Laozi said, "Tao patterns itself after its own nature. The delicious food seems tasteless." In ancient Chinese aesthetics, there were two styles of aesthetics—"lotus out of clear water" and "having eyes filled with engravings," but at least from the Southern and Northern dynasties, there had been a tendency to eagerly pursue a fresh and natural style. In the Southern dynasties, Tao Yuanming's poems were held in high esteem because they were both natural and transcendent. Later on, Xie Lingyun's poems were regarded as "incipient hibiscus, natural and loveable." Li Bai of the Tang Dynasty also said, "Out of clear water lotus engraved by nature." "Since the Jian'an Reign Period, flowery language has not been cherished. This wise dynasty restored the spirits of ancient times, plainness and purity are upheld." *Poetry Classified* by Sikong Tu wrote, "The beauty of the lotus out of the clear water lies in the fact that 'vital breath coming from afar, it was intuitively created by nature.'" It is obvious that their pursuit of aesthetics was based on Laozi's aesthetical thought—"Tao patterning itself after its own nature" and "returning to nature." How can this pursuit be realized then? Laozi's aesthetical thought suggested that first of all, the theory of the aesthetical mind should be established, which also had a far-reaching influence throughout the ages.

妙处不传，隐显叵测，认为这样就可以达到意趣无穷的效果。老子说："道法自然"，"大味无味"。中国古代美学思想中，虽然同时存在着"清水芙蓉"和"雕缋满眼"两种美学风格，但至少从南北朝开始，在中国的美学思想中，已经形成了更强烈追求清新自然的审美倾向。六朝时，先是陶渊明的诗因为自然超然而受到推崇，接着谢灵运的诗又被赏为"初发芙蓉，自然可爱"。唐代的李白也说："清水出芙蓉，天然去雕饰"；"自从建安来，绮丽不足珍，圣代复元古，垂衣贵清真。"司空图的《诗品》说："清水芙蓉"的美是："生气远出，妙造自然"。显然都是把老子的"道法自然"、返璞归真的美学思想，作为他们审美追求的依据的。而如何才能实现这种审美追求呢？老子美学思想中提出，首先必须建造一个审美心胸的理论，这一点也一直发挥着深远的影响。

图书在版编目(CIP)数据

老子:汉英对照/高华平著:汪榕培,曹盈,王善江译.
—南京:南京大学出版社,2010.3(2012.7重印)
(中国思想家评传简明读本)
ISBN 978-7-305-06607-8

Ⅰ.老… Ⅱ.①高…②汪…③曹…④王… Ⅲ.老子—
评传—汉、英 Ⅳ.B223.1

中国版本图书馆CIP数据核字(2009)第237561号

出 版 者 南京大学出版社
社 址 南京汉口路22号 邮 编 210093
网 址 http://www.NjupCo.com
出 版 人 左 健

丛 书 名 《中国思想家评传》简明读本(中英文版)
书 名 老 子
著 者 高华平
译 者 汪榕培 曹 盈 王善江
审 读 金 晶
责任编辑 李海霞 编辑热线 025-83685720

照 排 江苏凤凰制版印务中心
印 刷 江苏徐州新华印刷厂
开 本 787×1092 1/16 印张 11 字数 214千
版 次 2010年3月第1版 2012年7月第2次印刷
ISBN 978-7-305-06607-8
定 价 26.80元

发行热线 025-83594756
电子邮箱 Press@NjupCo.com
Sales@NjupCo.com (市场部)